FAN
PHEN**O**MENA

# THE
# HUNGER
# GAMES

## BY NICOLA BALKIND

Credits

First Published in the UK in 2014 by Intellect Books,
The Mill, Parnall Road, Fishponds, Bristol, BS16 3JG, UK

First Published in the USA in 2014 by Intellect Books,
The University of Chicago Press, 1427 E. 60th Street,
Chicago, IL 60637, USA

Copyright © 2014 Intellect Ltd

Author: Nicola Balkind

Series Editor and Design: Gabriel Solomons

Typesetting: Stephanie Sarlos

Copy Editor: Emma Rhys

A Catalogue record for this book is available from
the British Library

**Fan Phenomena Series**
ISSN: 2051-4468
eISSN: 2051-4476

**Fan Phenomena: The Hunger Games**
ISBN:  978-1-78320-204-1
eISBN:  978-1-78320-283-6 / 978-1-78320-284-3

Printed and bound by
Bell & Bain Limited, Glasgow

intellect

# Contents

# **Acknowledgements**

**Acknowledgements**

First, I'd like to express my gratitude to the tireless Gabriel Solomons and the entire Intellect team. My love and thanks, as ever, to my husband, Evan, for his boundless support and sharp eye. Thanks also to my mentors and great friends, the best pair of Paul Gs a young writer could have the luck to run into: Paul Gallagher and Paul Greenwood, for their help and support. Finally, I must thank my fantastic interviewees, without whom we wouldn't have a first-hand look at *The Hunger Games* fandom. Thanks all so much for your intelligence, warmth, and for pointing me in the right direction: the bright aca-fan V. Arrow, tireless reporter Sara Gundell, warm and whip-smart podcasters Adam Spunberg and Savanna New, and co-creators Samantha Sisson and Aaron Darcy. And thank you, the reader, for giving *Fan Phenomena: The Hunger Games* a go – now get to it!

# Introduction
# Nicola Balkind

→ In the scheme of fandom history, *The Hunger Games* and its fans, self-dubbed 'Tributes', are a brand new phenomenon. The meteoric success of Suzanne Collins's trilogy and its subsequent adaptation to film began only a handful of years ago in 2008, when Katniss Everdeen, The Tribute from District 12, was born. Her transformation into The Girl on Fire, a Star-Crossed Lover and, finally, the Mockingjay, was echoed IRL (in real life) as its cultural resonance became pop culture relevance.

The first print run of *The Hunger Games* was set at 50,000 and quickly quintupled, and five years on there are 26 million copies of The Hunger Games series books in print. All three instalments, *The Hunger Games*, *Catching Fire* and *Mockingjay* topped the *New York Times* Bestseller list; the series was voted second after Harry Potter (J.K. Rowling, 1997-2007) in NPR's (National Public Radio) top 100 YA (young adult) novels; and by 2012 the series has become the most-sold books on Amazon.com. It is a phenomenon which continues to grow, and is only half-way through its movie release schedule of four films. With each release, the fan base grows and the media's early comparisons of Part One to the likes of *Battle Royale* (Koushun Takami, 1996) and *The Long Walk* (Stephen King, 1979) seem to fall away as the series comes into its own. *The Hunger Games* (Gary Ross, 2012) made over $690 million globally, with the third-best domestic opening weekend of all time – best overall for a non-sequel. It still holds the latter title and its success paved the way for Part Two, *Catching Fire* (Francis Lawrence, 2013), which currently holds the sixth best opening weekend of all time behind only superheroes (Iron Man (*Iron Man 3*, Shane Black, 2013), Avengers (*The Avengers*, Joss Whedon, 2012) and the 'Dark Knight' Batman sequels (*The Dark Knight*, 2008 and *The Dark Knight Rises*, 2013 directed by Christopher Nolan), and wizards (*Harry Potter and the Deathly Hallows Part 2*, David Yates, 2011).

In 2008–09, a vibrant community had already begun to form and flourish around The Hunger Games series. Early adopters started to establish fansites, thoughtful readers discussed deeper readings and debated the issues presented within the books, and fan creators were populating fanfiction websites and blogging platforms with their transformative creations based on the series. Meanwhile fervour within the movie industry was growing as Nina Jacobson's production company Color Force beat out the competition and acquired the film rights in March 2009, which were then passed on to Lionsgate. Shortly after *Mockingjay* was published, Gary Ross was announced as director of *The Hunger Games* movie, and its release set for March 2012. Then Academy Award-nominated, now Oscar-winning Jennifer Lawrence was cast as Katniss Everdeen, a strong-willed, loyal teen who is deadly with a bow and arrow. (Think Joan of Arc meets Artemis and you're half-way there.)

While earlier Harry Potter and Twilight series set the stage for The Hunger Games's success, the series presents darker themes than its predecessors. Set in a dystopian future built upon the remains of North America, Panem exists under a totalitarian regime ruled by its Capitol, a gleaming centre of government and culture, surrounded by twelve Districts. Citizens outside the Capitol are oppressed due to an uprising and 'Dark Days' which took place 70-some years before Katniss's story begins. Themes of poverty, hunger, economic inequality and oppression are examined in detail, all of it centred around the annual spectacle known as the Hunger Games, in which all 12- to 18-year-olds are rounded up and one male and one female 'Tribute' from each District

## Introduction
Nicola Balkind

are chosen to fight to the death.

Some fantastic fan academics like V. Arrow and Valerie Estelle Frankel have written great volumes with in-depth textual analyses of Suzanne Collins's works. Smart Pop also published an essay collection taking in YA authors' favourite aspects of the series in book and film form in *The Girl Who Was on Fire* (2011). Others still have found angles and lenses through which to examine the series and its various facets. Our primary interest, though, is with the fans who have made the series such a pop culture success: those who have recognized its cultural relevance, amplified its resonance and expressed their own reverence for its issues, characters and spectacle.

In Chapter 1 we will introduce ourselves to Suzanne Collins as a fan, looking at the texts from which she drew her inspiration. Next we'll take a look at a couple of the bigger issues and their translation from book to film in Chapter 2 on 'War & Violence'. In Chapter 3, we will explore the greater context of women on film, why the meteoric success of *The Hunger Games* movie proved the viability of films with female leads, and the gender representations of Katniss as a 'strong female character'. As the marketing for this female-led franchise took hold, Lionsgate's message and those of the books appeared to be at odds, which is discussed at length in Chapter 4: 'Propos: The Publicity vs The Message'. Race and representation was also a contentious issue for fans, and we'll take a look at the greater debates that took place within the fandom in Chapter 5: 'Race & Representation in Panem & Beyond'. Despite these scuffles, positive messages are replete within the series, and in Chapter 6 we see the biggest issues interact with real life in the form of fan activism. It's not all serious though, as these YA fans are also a playful sort, creating spaces relating to The Hunger Games in the virtual world and in real life, which you can sample in Chapter 7. Fans and the studio don't always see eye to eye, so Chapter 8 looks at one fan project which rocked the boat in 'The Fans vs The Man: The Capitol PN vs Panem October'. Finally, our overview of The Hunger Games fandom culminates in Chapter 9, a bumper chapter which takes in the landscape of fan creation from simple recreations to brand-new worlds.

Go forth, dear reader, and sample it all as though at a Capitol feast. And, as ever, may the odds be *ever* in your favour. ●

# MAY THE ODDS
# BE EVER
# IN YOUR FAVOR!

**EFFIE TRINKET**
THE HUNGER GAMES

Chapter
1

# The Hunger Games 101: Suzanne as a Fan & the Author's Influences

→ Like all great dystopias, The Hunger Games is informed by elements from contemporary society. While writing the series, Suzanne Collins was concerned with a number of issues including the impact of the media on children's lives, dangerous decisions made by governments, and poverty. The publicity-shy author describes her creation of the story thus:

Fig. 1: Suzanne Collins

I was channel surfing between reality TV programming and actual war coverage when Katniss's story came to me. One night I'm sitting there flipping around and on one channel there's a group of young people competing for, I don't know, money maybe? And on the next, there's a group of young people fighting an actual war. And I was tired, and the lines began to blur in this very unsettling way, and I thought of this story. (Scholastic Book Club)

Suzanne Collins's influences in creating The Hunger Games contributed to a publishing marvel. In 2006, she pitched a duology to Scholastic under the working title 'The Tribute of District 12'. Scholastic immediately signed the author to a six-figure, two-book deal – which quickly became a trilogy. This initial book deal – the story of one girl from a small District in the futuristic society of Panem – was the seed of a cultural phenomenon and spectacle worthy of the Capitol itself. Since the first instalment was published in 2008, Suzanne Collins has become one of the world's top-ten highest-earning authors; The Hunger Games movie has earned worldwide box office takings exceeding $690 million; and the series has garnered hordes of fans – calling themselves 'Tributes' – who have made the story their own.

Age-wise, The Hunger Games protagonist Katniss Everdeen is fairly representative of Collins's target audience. Katniss is our window into the world of Panem – she guides us through the story, sharing her experience first-hand, in engaging present tense narration. She is not an explicitly unreliable narrator, and all that remains unknown to the audience is that which Katniss does not discuss, describe, or explain. We can learn more about that which she does not describe, and the greater cultural context that she inhabits, through examination of the author's influences. In a Scholastic Q&A, Collins was posed the following question: 'What do you want young readers to take away from the books?' She answered that she would want readers to think about whether they are taking their next meal for granted while others starve, and to ask questions about the choices that their government or governments around the world make. 'What's your relationship to reality TV versus the news?' she asks her readers. 'Was there anything in the news that disturbed you because they related to your own life, and if there was, what can you do about it?' Collins's ideas about how she wants her reader to relate to The Hunger Games are key.

So are fans, young and otherwise, taking away these key messages from The Hunger Games books? In order to understand the series, and any works of art, including fanworks, which use it as a source of inspiration, we must first seek to understand the author's reverence of her source material. Collins's unique blending of Greek myth and modern war stories are a refreshing take on the modern-day issues. Child soldiers and the impact of reality television and propagandistic media on young people are explored in an arena created for young people, placing them at the centre of the action and the

The Hunger Games 101: Suzanne as a Fan & the Author's Influences

*Fig. 2: Katniss Everdeen*

*Fig. 3: Katniss volunteers in place of her sister, Primrose.*

issue. Many critics have cited the opposition that Collins sets up between reality television and war coverage with the suggestion that this story explores the possibility of reality TV being taken to its furthest, darkest conclusion. Collins's work poses this question: What is real, and what is entertainment?

That being said, Collins's source material is not unusual. Reaching back to Greek mythology, the foundational concept in The Hunger Games is based upon the story of 'Theseus and the Minotaur'. There are many variations of the tale, but the key event is King Minós of Crete ordering that Athens must make Tribute, with seven girls and seven boys aged 8 to 14 to be sacrificed to the city, every nine years, and be placed into the labyrinth of the Minotaur. Tributes are chosen by selecting shards of pottery from a basket: those who draw a piece marked with an X are the chosen ones. Their fate is a terrifying battle to the death where none have been known to survive. Theseus puts himself in place of a Tribute – a young girl, no less – with plans to sacrifice himself. But he emerges a victor, saving the life of the child Aktaíans in the process. In the myth, Agaeus of Athens wonders how many draws it will take until his people rise up in rebellion. The rebels of The Hunger Games's Districts wonder the same – and, where the story begins, 74 years after the end of the Dark Days and into the rule of Panem's Capitol government, the residents of this dystopian future finally have an answer.

In a Q&A with Scholastic, Collins says,

A significant influence would have to be the Greek myth of Theseus and the Minotaur. The myth tells [of] punishment for past deeds […] [and] even as a kid, I could appreciate how ruthless this was. Crete was sending a very clear message: 'Mess with us and we'll do something worse than kill you. We'll kill your children.' And the thing is, it was allowed; the parents sat by powerless to stop it. Theseus, who was the son of the king, volunteered to go. I guess in her own way, Katniss is a futuristic Theseus. In keeping with the classical roots, I send my tributes into an updated version of the Roman gladiator games, which entails a ruthless government forcing people to fight to the death as popular entertainment.

Like Theseus, Katniss volunteers as Tribute. Some translations of the myth see Theseus take the place of a particularly sweet, small, innocent young girl, who is terrified at her fate. Rather than seeking the Minotaur at the heart of the Labyrinth, as Theseus does, Katniss's motivation is to protect that which she loves most: she is sacrificing herself to save her younger sister, Prim. Like Theseus, she leads many Tributes to safety, forging alliances and joining forces with Peeta against the Gamemakers and President Snow (who could be read as King Minós, and the Muttations with which he fills his Arena, the Minotaur). Each Tribute is deadly, but none so much as the Capitol's wrath. As the author indicates above, Collins's Capitol sends the same message to its Districts as Crete did the Aktaíans.

Katniss's overall trajectory throughout the series can also be compared with the historical Thracian gladiator Spartacus. Like Katniss, Spartacus transforms from slave to gladiator, gladiator to rebel, then rebel to face of a war. Spartacus' rebellion led to the Third Servile War with the Roman Empire, mirroring Panem's second major rebellion led by the Mockingjay.

*Panem et Circences* is at the root of the name of the fictional country where our story is set: Panem. From the Roman for 'Bread and Circuses', this refers to the exchange of entertainment for the needs or wants of the populous. Give them bread and circuses

Fig. 4: A fan's rendering of the Capitol.

and they'll do anything. These reciprocal factors are at the centre of Collins's entire notion of war and reality television – particularly the latter. In order to have entertainment, the people must sacrifice themselves. In order to have food, they must sacrifice their freedoms and risk their lives. A meagre year's worth of grain and oil is known as Tessera (or in plural, Tesserae), and is exchanged for another token in the draw for the person who claims it. In Panem, the children of the Districts must sacrifice themselves in this way and increase their odds of becoming unwilling contenders in this brutal form of entertainment. Like the Aktaíans, their names are drawn from a random lottery known as the Reaping.

The Capitol also takes on a number of Roman influences, from its excesses to the names of its population. 'The world of Panem, particularly the Capitol, is loaded with Roman references,' Collins tells Scholastic, and this is clear to see from the moment Katniss sets foot in the Capitol. Capitol citizens, and particularly its leaders, resemble those of the Roman set: Roman Emperors and their allies. 'Gamemakers' fight their way to the top of this white-collar gladiatorial race. Just as Tributes turned Victors become celebrities, Gamemakers are the brains behind the Hunger Games – they are the television makers, the cogs in the machine of the Capitol's *Panem et Circences* regime. Children in the adjoining, richer Districts 1 and 2, often known as 'Career Tributes' or simply 'Careers' on account of their pre-Hunger Games military training, also boast gladiatorial Roman names, or simply gauche ones like Marvel and Cato, Glimmer and Clove.

The Gamemakers and Capitol citizens' names refer to the likes of Julius Caesar (Caesar Flickerman, the host of the Hunger Games); the philosopher Seneca (Seneca Crane, head Gamemaker); counsel of the Roman Republic, Lucius Cornelius Cinna (Cinna, Katniss's stylist and potential rebel); and Career Tribute Cato (Cato the Younger, stubborn and tenacious political statesmen of the late Roman Republic). Fan books like 2012's *The Panem Companion* by V. Arrow and *Katniss the Cattail* by Valerie E. Frankel look into these names and their meanings in great detail. For our purposes, even a quick skim over these names and their potential meanings demonstrates a great interest and influence of Roman names and culture on the part of Suzanne Collins.

Some the author's favourite novels also hold references that can be interpreted as influences. Collins herself has pointed to Bathsheeba Everdene, the lead character from Thomas Hardy's *Far From the Madding Crowd* (1874) as one inspiration for the name Katniss Everdeen. She has listed some of her favourite novels for Scholastic, which included a mention of *Dandelion Wine* (1957) by Ray Bradbury – a possible reference to Peeta as Katniss's dandelion, her reminder that spring, and better, more prosperous days would come.

Collins has cited the formative years she spent away from home in Grades 7–10 as a time when she came to love some of her favourite novels, including *A Tree Grows in Brooklyn* (1943) by Betty Smith and *A Wrinkle in Time* (1962) by Madeleine L'Engle. 'I'm sure that the choice to make coal mining District 12's industry had to be influenced by Emile Zola's *Germinal*, [1885]' she told This is Teen in an interview prior to the release of *Mockingjay*.

Characters from the outer Districts are often named in direct opposition to those of the Capitol and Careers. The natural, plant-like and healing names of Katniss, her family, friends and allies seems to correspond with Collins's interest in her father's dabbling in edible plants. Katniss, or *Sagittaria*, is an aquatic root plant – she quips that her father told her that 'as long as you can find yourself, you'll never starve'. Appropriately, *Sagittaria* is also known as 'arrowhead'. Her sister, Primrose, is fairly self-explanatory. Katniss's ally in the Arena, Rue, takes her name from a small mountain flower, *Ruta graveolens*, and she demonstrates knowledge of healing plants to save Katniss. Rue hails from District 11, a harvesting District, where her fellow Tribute is named Thresh – the action of separating grain from wheat. This direct opposition between earthy, home-grown names and those of Roman gladiators and wartime thinkers sets up a clear opposition. While Collins deals with the blurring of boundaries, some of her further influences are also crystal clear.

As well as wartime thinkers, Collins is also concerned with the question of war itself: modern wars and who fights them, how this is orchestrated, and how we watch this narrative as it is played out in something close to realtime. Flipping, as Collins was, through television channels can blur the boundaries between truth and fiction. How do we tell the difference between real-life war coverage versus a film about the war? How does this differ, morally and aesthetically, to an advert for a popular war-themed video game or, say, a reality show about the lives of troops? In her video with This is Teen, Suzanne Collins notes:

> There's this potential for desensitising the audience so that when they see real tragedy playing out on the news, it doesn't have the impact it should. It all just blurs into one program. I think it's very important not just for young people, but for adults to make sure they're making the distinction. Because the young soldiers dying in the war in Iraq, it's not going to end at the commercial break, it's not something fabricated, it's not a game, it's your life.

We, as readers, are given a privileged position within the storyworld of The Hunger Games; a unique insight into the experience of one Citizen of Panem. We read Katniss's thoughts in first person, a realtime, present tense, internal dialogue. By experiencing the Games through the eyes of a Tribute we are also given another vantage point: that of the close family member of a Tribute. We become privy to Katniss's thoughts, actions and reactions; but are also put in the place of a family member losing a sibling to the Reaping, a friend and neighbour, and someone who owes a debt of gratitude in a hard and desperate world. Katniss's perspective looks out to all of these viewpoints, and infers enough for us to imagine the rest. From Katniss's perspective, we are invited to deride Capitol citizens – though later, when she learns their own struggles, many become humanized and we are invited to empathize with their plight. This position allows and facilitates empathy with Panem citizens of all creeds: those who, like Katniss, are too poor to fend for themselves claim Tesserae and find other means for survival. Katniss's mother, a widow, represents women marginalized further from a broken society, while Gale's mother bears the burden of many children and Gale a forced adulthood. Madge Undersee, the Mayor's daughter, is also presented as a suffering member of the upper class. Despite being sheltered compared with Katniss, Madge is far from immune to the Capitol's wrath. And still they are greeted with the Capitol's sing-song well-wishes, 'May the odds be ever in your favour.'

A position of empathy is imperative in the setting-up of this tale and exploration of fact versus fiction. Within the story these strands are shown from Katniss's perspective and the Hunger Games events deviate from what we – or at least Katniss – know to be true. We never hear the first names of Katniss's parents, or Gale's father, for example. What's important is that by experiencing the world through Katniss's eyes, and just as the Districts become drawn to her as a (literally) fiery beacon, readers and characters alike rally around Katniss as a sole source of hope. We discover that even before she entered the Games, townsfolk admired her tenacity and strength, and it is with this power that she earns herself sponsors in the Arena. She is there to sacrifice herself in place of her family, and this becomes a major theme.

The importance of family rings true throughout the books, as does the way the author handles such dark subject matter in a story aimed at teens. In interviews, Suzanne Collins cites her father's experiences growing up during the Depression and involvement as a serviceman during the Vietnam War, and these influences are clear. When asked in a Scholastic Q&A what drew her to such serious subject matters as poverty, starvation, oppression and the effects of war upon others, she answered:

That was probably my dad's influence. He was career Air Force, a military specialist, a historian, and a doctor of political science. When I was a kid, he was gone for a year in Vietnam. It was very important to him that we understood about certain aspects of life. So, it wasn't enough to visit a battlefield, we needed to know why the battle occurred, how it played out, and the consequences. Fortunately, he had a gift for presenting history as a fascinating story. He also seemed to have a good sense of exactly how much a child could handle, which is quite a bit.

*Fig. 5: Katniss Everdeen*

More specifically, she also cites his experiences close to the breadline:

> Some things I knew from listening to my dad talking about his childhood. He grew up during the Depression. For his family, hunting was not a sport but a way to put meat on the table. He also knew a certain amount about edible plants [...] I also read a big stack of wilderness survival guidebooks. And here's what I learned: you've got to be really good to survive out there for more than a few days.

Sound familiar?

Collins's life was greatly affected by war and the military. Her father served in the Vietnam War, was absent throughout her life, and later suffered from the symptoms of post-traumatic stress disorder. These experiences are echoed in Collins's books. In the author's first novel series, Gregor the Overlander (2003-2007), the titular protagonist suffers the absence of a father. Katniss also mourns the loss of her late father and, after participating in the Hunger Games, suffers from PTSD. One *New York Times* preview also includes Collins reflecting upon her father's recitation of poet Lieutenant Colonel John McCrae's 'In Flanders Fields' (1915) to her as a child: a poem whose larks may be a precursor of the symbolic songbird, the Mockingjay. As is clear in both the Gregor the Overlander series and The Hunger Games trilogy, Collins follows her father's impulse to educate young people about the realities of war. 'If we wait too long, what kind of expectation can we have?' she said in an interview with the *New York Times*. 'We think we're sheltering them, but what we're doing is putting them at a disadvantage.'

If there is one thing we can take away from this inspection of Suzanne Collins's influences, it is that they combined to create a narrative that sought to teach children about key issues like war and injustice, and that resulted in an enormous cultural phenomenon. Just as Suzanne Collins's influences came together to create The Hunger Games and its plot, characters, history and culture, readers and fans thresh these seeds from the story to create their own works of art – including drawings, costumes, food, fiction and song. In Chapter 2 we'll look at how these issues of war and violence are reflected in the cultural discussion surrounding The Hunger Games series. ●

The Hunger Games 101: Suzanne as a Fan & the Author's Influences

~~~~~~~~~~

## GO FURTHER

### Books

The Panem Companion: From Mellark Bakery to Mockingjays
V. Arrow
(Dallas: Smart Pop Books, 2012)

*Katniss the Cattail: An Unauthorized Guide to Names and Symbols in Suzanne Collins'*
*The Hunger Games*
Valerie Estelle Frankel
(Seattle: CreateSpace Independent Publishing Platform, 2012)

### Extracts/Essays/Articles

'An Interview with Suzanne Collins'
James Blasingame and Suzanne Collins
In *Journal of Adolescent & Adult Literacy*. 52. 8 (2009), pp. 726–27 [Online], http://
www.jstor.org/stable/27654337.

### Online

*Suzanne Collins Q&A with Scholastic* [n.d.], http://www.scholastic.com/thehunger-
games/media/suzanne_collins_q_and_a.pdf.

Interview with Suzanne Collins
*Scholastic International School Book Club* [n.d.],
http://world.clubs-kids.scholastic.co.uk/clubs_content/18832

'Q&A with Hunger Games Author Suzanne Collins'
Hannah Trierweiler Hudson
*Scholastic.com* [n.d.], http://www.scholastic.com/teachers/article/qa-hunger-games-
author-suzanne-collins.

'What came before "The Hunger Games"'
Andrew O'Hehir
*Salon*. 14 March 2012, http://www.salon.com/2012/03/14/what_came_before_the_hun-
ger_games/.

'Hunger Games Glossary'
Amanda Bell
*Next Movie.* 7 March 2012,
http://www.nextmovie.com/blog/hunger-games-glossary/.

'Suzanne Collins' War Stories For Kids'
Susan Dominus
*New York Times.* 8 April 2011,
http://www.nytimes.com/2011/04/10/magazine/mag-10collins-t.
html?pagewanted=3&_r=1.

'Suzanne Collins Answers Questions About the Hunger Games'
*This is Teen* [YouTube]
2 September 2010, http://www.youtube.com/watch?v=FH15DI8ZW14.

'Suzanne Collins on the books she loves'
Tina Jordan
*Entertainment Weekly.* 12 August 2010,
http://shelf-life.ew.com/2010/08/12/suzanne-collins-on-the-books-she-loves/.

'A Killer Story: An Interview with Suzanne Collins, Author of "The Hunger Games"'
Rick Margolis
*School Library Journal.* 1 September 2008,
http://www.slj.com/2008/09/authors-illustrators/a-killer-story-an-interview-with-suzanne-collins-author-of-the-hunger-games/.

'Suzanne Collins' War Stories For Kids'
Susan Dominus
*New York Times.* 8 April 2011,
http://www.nytimes.com/2011/04/10/magazine/mag-10collins-t.
html?pagewanted=3&_r=1

# Chapter
2

# Hunger For The Games: War & Violence

→ The Hunger Games is unlike most of its YA (young adult) dystopian counterparts because it tackles myriad complex issues head-on, most significantly violence against children. This has caused widespread media debate about the effects of these messages on its fans and, more generally, impressionable teenaged readers.

*Fig. 1: Fan Art of Katniss in the Arena.*

This chapter will look at what kind of violence is portrayed in the series, some key elements which were successfully adapted from book to film, and some theories and commentary surrounding the ways in which these issues have, and will, play out in the media. The Capitol enforces violence on children, but more specifically it mandates violence of children against other children. This is one of the most contentious issues in the series, particularly in its translation from page to screen. How does a movie studio portray child-on-child violence and get away with it? What purpose does it serve? And is there a place for these issues on-screen? First we'll look at the Capitol's violent means, particularly those ideas and elements within the books that fans were most eager or curious

## Hunger For The Games: War & Violence

*Fig. 2: Katniss and Peeta escorted to the Reaping by Peacekeepers in Catching Fire.*

to see adapted to screen. Then we will examine how these ideas translated into a visual medium, how this fits in the cultural milieu, and some key reactions.

Panem is a country in lock-down. Its centre of wealth and government, the Capitol, wields oppressive economic power over its entire citizenship. By keeping each of its twelve Districts distinct, discrete, and out of reach of its neighbours, the Capitol holds inordinate power over its people. There is no communication between Districts, creating a population that is ignorant of the lives and customs of its neighbours and is conditioned to hate them based on their performance in the annual Hunger Games spectacle. Each District lives under the watchful eyes of Capitol Peacekeepers as part of a system that keeps the economy small and unable to grow, in which the odds are stacked against every family and, specifically, every child. The economics of Panem come into play here; however it is through the Capitol's systematic oppression of and violence towards the District people that many of the story's darker themes bubble to the surface. The annual Hunger Games is a form of entertainment for the Capitol, terrorism for the Districts, and a constant reminder to all that a step out of line means certain death. What is more terrifying is that the Capitol won't kill you; it will kill your children.

Warfare from the Capitol comes in many forms, chiefly brutal (physical) and psychological. Physical aggression is usually channelled through an intermediary source, sent out by the Capitol to attack while the powerful elite dine and socialize. Intermediary aggressors come in the form of Peacekeepers, other Tributes, the Arena, and Muttations. The latter two are both physically and psychologically aggressive, and are employed as a form of psychological warfare. Peacekeepers are easily portrayed on-screen. Their white uniforms and masks make them faceless, armoured Stormtrooper-esque attack dogs of the law. Other Tributes and the Arena are the aggressors most seen in *The Hunger Games* movie, with Careers posing an added threat due to their comparative skill and training to kill. Fire is a key weapon of the Capitol in the Arena itself – which is also home to the deadly Muttations. The Muttations in the 74th Hunger Games wear the eyes of fallen Tributes; the Quarter Quell's Jabberjays' voices are filled with the screams of loved ones; and the Capitol is always devising ways to break Katniss's spirit. Some of these aggressive and psychological forms can also be symbolic: for example, Snow leaves Katniss a single rose as a token of his presence in her home; an invasion of privacy so absolute that it leaves behind a literal, lingering stench. Peeta's torture is specifically psychological, erasing what he knows and implanting false memories which make him see Katniss as the enemy.

The film-makers' visualizations of the Arenas and Muttations were among the most anticipated portrayals that fans awaited seeing translated to screen. At the time of writing, we still await films three and four – *Mockingjay* Parts One and Two – to see how the film-makers deal with one major question on fans' minds: is Gale responsible for Prim's death? But first, how did the media react to violence in *The Hunger Games*?

## The Hunger Games

Mainstream media, news websites and blogs all reported on a key issue of *The Hunger Games* film adaptation: the representation of violence against, and between, children. Hands were wrung, Lionsgate made secret plans to test the market before revealing more violent trailers, and commentators like Slate were already speculating over how the studio would pull off portrayals of child soldiers and warfare in *Mockingjay*.

First, let's look at the cultural ideas that Suzanne Collins presented and responded to. She is concerned with the impact of mainstream media including reality television, images of war, and the blurred distinction that is created by the juxtaposition of the two. While these issues aren't unique to the 2010s in particular, some other aspects of the time are, including the climate into which the books were born. Historically, recession times have led to a rise in dystopias. We've seen it time and time again: think of the heyday of George Orwell's *Nineteen Eighty-Four* (1949) and Aldous Huxley's *Brave New World* (1932). Today the United States has been at war for over a decade, which prompted Amy Davidson to ask, 'is it really a coincidence that the biggest movie of the year is the first in a trilogy in which torture, terror, asymmetric warfare, and the manipulation of public opinion all play a role?'

The media has hungrily dissected the popularity of Collins's book series. In an article entitled 'Fresh Hell' published in June 2010, Davidson's *New Yorker* colleague Laura Miller also sought to find the seed of *The Hunger Games*'s success. She takes a broad focus, looking at the wider cultural backdrop against which its release played out. As Miller points out, The Hunger Games is a key contributor to the boom of dystopian YA fiction. Miller also cites similar dystopian worlds: books like James Dashner's The Maze Runner series (2009-2012) and Veronica Roth's Divergent trilogy (2011-2013). Their protagonists are strong, smart and versatile, finding ways out of the labyrinth using their individual smarts or a 'special' talent. Katniss's hunting skills keep her alive, become her greatest weapon, and contribute to her transformation into the symbol of a revolution. All three series' protagonists also narrate in first person, giving realtime insights into their experiences. Ultimately, all three diverge from the dystopian genre and form as we

Hunger For The Games: War & Violence

Fig. 3. Mockingjay graffiti
featured in the Catching Fire
movie.

knew it in the aforementioned 1940s classics.

One major theme that sets The Hunger Games, and particularly *Mockingjay*, apart from these dystopian classics is hope. On the whole, these teen-focused dystopias are far more hopeful than their adult fiction counterparts. Unlike Orwell and his contemporaries' warning sirens and lessons on lost morality, The Hunger Games reads less like a cautionary tale on the dangers of reality television and more like a high drama about its (perhaps inevitable) dark conclusion. Miller takes this line of inquiry further, seeking to outline key differences in the way these stories are handled for different age groups, and how information technology and communication play into the story. In The Hunger Games series, communication issues are primarily of the propagandist variety. Unlike many of Miller's example texts, Collins's series does not introduce a seeming utopia which slowly shows its true colours. Katniss's narration portrays its dark history from the beginning, unravelling the depths of institutional depravity in a way that allows the reader to learn about the world through and with Katniss. Though we know that the Capitol is evil, the details of its wiles emerge with time. Without suggesting that our governments are capable of the same evils as the Capitol, there are plenty of moments that draw parallels with the present day. As Davidson points out,

> The teen-agers who love these books are watching stories in the news, and thinking about them, and should be given some credit for drawing connections. It is hard to imagine that a child who read and loved 'The Hunger Games' wouldn't have had some of its images in mind when forwarding around the Kony 2012 video, and vice versa.

These connections are an important part of the reading process. Katniss herself is remarkably media-literate, ever observant and always analysing the way in which her story will be portrayed, especially the parts that the Capitol edits out. What is most stark about The Hunger Games in this instance is not necessarily the messages about reality TV or propaganda, but its portrayal of the Capitol's treatment of its own people. Katniss uses the propaganda machine to turn the Capitol's message on its head, and in doing so she sparks an uprising and a new political era for Panem.

One fan at Victor's Village, a Hunger Games fansite, wrote a piece in defence of the violent issues broached in the series and how Collins portrays them. The writer's age is unclear, but since they refer to a team practice and an adult figure, one would deduce that he or she is probably a teenager. Rue's Melody writes:

> The main argument I hear against the books is that they are violent, glorify violence, and are all about violence. However, these books are a far cry from this preconceived notion [...] Collins' books do everything to completely remove any sort of 'glory' from the violence [...] The Hunger Games is about the value of life, and fighting to stay

grounded. The Hunger Games is about preserving ethics and morality in a society devoid of both.

The story of The Hunger Games also focuses on a new generation, not the established adults of society. Young people are victims of the Capitol's greatest crimes. They also represent the unlikely spark of hope during dark times that have lasted over 75 years – long enough that few, if any, remember a time before the Capitol reign and the annual fanfare of the Hunger Games. Although they represent Capitol evil, even the deadly Career Tributes can ultimately be empathized with as children and victims. In the book, 'othering' – seeing or defining undesirable characters as 'other' – is a key way in which these relationships are managed. As Satsuma, another contributor to *Victor's Village*, writes in 'Will The Real Katniss Everdeen Please Stand Up? Part 2':

> When Gale visits Katniss post-reaping in THG, he compares the Games to hunting animals, and Katniss admits internally that 'if I can forget they're people, it will be no different at all' (THG Ch.3). At first, she finds the prep team to be 'so unlike people that I'm no more self-conscious than if a trio of oddly colored birds were pecking around my feet'. On the other side, Flavius says post-Remake, 'You almost look like a human being now!' (THG Ch.5) What a microcosm of the tendency to dehumanize the 'other' on both sides of the Capitol-District divide. In CF, even Peeta is disgusted when the 'preps' encourage them to essentially binge and purge. Yet, when Katniss finds her prep team imprisoned in D13, she is appalled, and demands they be set free.

Empathy is also used as a tool to ensure that child-on-child violence is never condoned. As Davidson writes in the *New Yorker*:

> All three books are full of the killings of young people, but also with an exceptional sense of outrage at their loss. The deaths aren't cartoonish; they stay with you the way that fairy-tale deaths do, but with the reflection the prince or miller's daughter tends to lack about the psychic cost of being the one doing the killing. That was on the printed page, though, where it is far easier to allude to what is seen and then talk about why you wish you had never caught a glimpse.

Speaking of catching glimpses of violent deaths, the hardcore Hunger Games fans waited with bated breath for the initial movie trailer, keen to see how the Games would play out, what the Arena would look like, and how the terrifying Muttations would look without the help of these literary techniques. Meanwhile, Lionsgate was playing its own tactical marketing game as they tested the ground to see how little Hunger Games action they could include in the trailer. This served to test how much audiences could bear to be withheld but also demonstrates that the framing is a particularly important

*Fig. 4: Fan Art of Katniss in Mockingjay.*

indicator of what the studio thought audiences would find socially acceptable. According to Brooks Barnes' report for the *New York Times*, Lionsgate's chief marketing officer, Tim Palen, originally did not want any of the Games to be shown in trailers: 'We made a rule that we would never say, "23 kids get killed." We say, "only one wins."' This strategy of withholding fight scenes from trailers has prevailed throughout the marketing of *Catching Fire*. While this may whet the fans' appetites, it also puts them in the position of a Capitol audience. This makes the movie more comfortable as pure entertainment and less powerful as an anti-war statement. *Feminist Frequency*'s Anita Sarkeesian pointed out one such failure in direction during *The Hunger Games* as the audience laughed upon Clove's death. If the movie fails in this arena, it dilutes the author's message and appears to condone violence against children.

Much like *The Hunger Games* film, *Catching Fire* takes place in District 12, the Capitol and the Hunger Games Arena. However, looking forward to the final act of the trilogy, *Mockingjay* takes place largely in the 'real' Panem rather than the Arena. It deals with darker themes relating to counterinsurgency, war, and real violence against children. *Slate* writer Erik Sofge was one of the first to consider the possibilities about how this would be portrayed and perceived on-screen. According to *Slate*, Hollywood takes three distinct approaches to similar science fiction or fantasy movies which appeal to a young audience and deal with sensitive subject matter. The approaches are outlined thus: (1) Play Chicken; (2) The Tactical Rewrite; or (3) Screw the Fanboys. Erik Sofge writes, 'Whatever *Mockingjay* is—a bold and unflinching climax to a best-selling series or a disjointed leap into antiwar protest fiction—there's one thing it probably isn't: a book that's easily adapted for the screen.'

The author draws on examples of scenes from similar films like *Twilight* (Catherine Hardwicke, 2008):

> If Lionsgate decides to play chicken with 'Mockingjay' in similar fashion, the studio would ditch the soapy trappings of the first two instalments and launch into a parade of gun battles right out of Starship Troopers, and end the entire franchise with its heroine a scarred, post-traumatic husk of her former self. A bluntly faithful adaptation might be a cinematic mess, but the true believers would flood the box office with their gratitude.

The movie adaptation of *Catching Fire* is incredibly faithful, suggesting that Lionsgate hoped to please the fans. However, even blunt faithfulness to the source text requires inspiration and visual references which make sense to the film's audience. A *Victor's Village* author who goes by the user name of Them There Eyes (themthereeyes1) presents a parallel which could serve as an interesting counterpoint to scenes within *Mockingjay*. This writer compares the Mockingjay riots with the peak of the Civil Rights Movement in the United States, including Martin Luther King Jr.'s 'I Have a Dream' speech. The author also has some interesting ideas about Katniss as a King-esque character. Parallels are drawn thus:

> Both [...] were leaders in highly publicized, fraught, and dangerous movements that were focused on the betterment of their country's functionality as a civil, equal, and productive societies [sic]. Both made great speeches in front [of] mass amounts of people, both came from dissimilar but still humble beginnings, and both were wounded, or in the unfortunate case of Mr. King Jr. assassinated in the process of participating in his cause.

This comparison with the Civil Rights movements gives us some ideas about the visual reference points which may be used to portray the riots and rebellion scenes in *Mockingjay*. This also suggests some powerful ways in which the Districts and, perhaps more importantly, the Panem media might interact with Katniss on its own stage. While Martin Luther King Jr. was a strict pacifist, Katniss resorts to violence often; but, at least initially, only to save her own life. In *Catching Fire* she deals with her guilt over the deaths she caused in the Hunger Games, but her actions in *Mockingjay*, while often sympathetic, are comparatively cut-throat. Collins uses Katniss's bows and arrows to demonstrate this change: in *The Hunger Games* she uses a wooden bow made by her father for survival, to hunt; in the Games itself and the Quarter Quell she uses the Capitol's silver finery, designed to kill; then finally, in *Mockingjay*, District 13 provides her with a black bow built only for destruction. This is another issue that Lionsgate must face: how to turn Katniss into more of a cold-blooded killer, demonstrating that she is not a moralist like Peeta and portraying her struggle during the final vote to continue or end the Hunger Games at the dawn of the new regime.

As mentioned above, another deeper issue from the book includes the aforementioned fan theories of Gale's part in Prim's untimely death. While we're encouraged to despise the Capitol, rebel warfare, particularly that of District 13, is a more complex evil. While Katniss needs their help to lead the rebellion against the Capitol, their goals and preferred methods are at odds. But Katniss and Coin need each other, and Gale is a complicating factor. Gale falls in with District 13, embracing warfare and causing his and Katniss's views to diverge, which puts strain on their relationship. If Lionsgate does decide to include the storyline about the rebel's bombs, (which first detonate to kill, then trigger a second time to claim a second round of victims, usually first responders) the way in which this plays out will be a sensitive issue for the film-makers and the audience.

Hunger For The Games: War & Violence

The portrayal of this storyline on-screen will require a great deal of tact, and will almost certainly fall under scrutiny. In the chapter 'Accountability for Acts of War in The Hunger Games' in V. Arrow's book *The Panem Companion* (2012), the author outlines the fan theories which relate to this issue. She poses this question: 'Who killed Prim Everdeen?'

> Although there are no definitive answers – the culprit behind Prim's death is never clearly revealed – different stances on the part of different groups of fans, and where they place the blame, play into differing ideas about morality in war as a whole. Who is to blame when it comes to the atrocities of war? The weapons' makers or the ones responsible for deploying them? The people who drove the necessity for war to begin with?

This presents an enormous question on the part of the film-makers. While answers range from the Capitol for starting the war; District 13 for likely detonating the bomb in a bid to make the Capitol look worse; and Beetee and/or Gale for potentially having created the bomb, the question is whether the movie will address this issue at all. Only time will tell, but if they are successful, Amy Davidson's words will apply to the films just as well as the books:

> [Katniss] basically spends three books mulling over the realization all children have that death is real, and irrevocable. (One problem, as Collins makes clear, is that Katniss, for most of the series, hasn't had the same revelation about the solidity of love.) She is able to be the moral center of the story because, as the plot becomes increasingly political, and the other characters are caught up in tactical discussions and propaganda campaigns and battle plans, she hasn't been able to get over her amazement at that simple truth. Maybe no one should.

Reading The Hunger Games series, it is clear that every use of violence is a condemnation of the act; but this intent does not always translate to screen. In the books, violence against and between children is dealt with head-on, without gore but with empathy and reverence. This poses a huge moral problem for the film-makers, who must attempt to portray violence in a way that is suitable for its target audience and which maintains Collins's subtle commentary. While the first film gained 12A and PG-13 ratings in its largest English-speaking markets, the fact remains that, in marketing the films, the studio has kept violence in its back pocket as a way to heighten the hype. While most commentators seem to agree that violence has been well served in the series so far, only time will tell how these key issues from the book of *Mockingjay* will play out on the big screen. Will Lionsgate reveal who killed Primrose Everdeen? ●

~~~~~~~~~~~

**GO FURTHER**

**Books**

*The Panem Companion: From Mellark Bakery to Mockingjays*
V. Arrow
(Dallas: Smart Pop Books, 2012)

**Online**

'Fifty Years Ago Today'
Them There Eyes
*Victor's Village*. 28 August 2013,
http://victorsvillage.com/2013/08/28/fifty-years-ago-today/.

'The Hunger Games Movie vs. the Book'
Anita Sarkeesian
*Feminist Frequency*. 12 April 2012,
http://www.feministfrequency.com/2012/04/the-hunger-game-a-book-and-movie-comparison/.

'Counterinsurgency and The Hunger Games'
Amy Davidson
*New Yorker*. 21 March 2012,
http://www.newyorker.com/online/blogs/comment/2012/03/hunger-games-and-counterinsurgency.html.

'How Will They Make a Movie out of Mockingjay?'
Erik Sofge
*Slate*. 21 March 2012,
http://www.slate.com/articles/arts/culturebox/2012/03/hunger_games_trilogy_how_will_they_make_a_movie_out_of_mockingjay_.single.html.

'How 'Hunger Games' Built Up Must-See Fever'
Brooks Barnes
*New York Times*. 19 March 2012,
http://www.nytimes.com/2012/03/19/business/media/how-hunger-games-built-up-must-see-fever.html?pagewanted=all.

'Don't Judge The Hunger Games Until You've Read It'
Rue's Melody
*Victor's Village.* 8 April 2012,
http://victorsvillage.com/2012/04/08/dont-judge-the-hunger-games-until-youve-read-it/.

'Will The Real Katniss Everdeen Please Stand Up? Part 2'
Satsuma
*Victor's Village.* 21 January 2013,
http://victorsvillage.com/2013/01/21/will-the-real-katniss-everdeen-please-stand-up-part-2/

'What Occupy can learn from the Hunger Games'
Mike Doherty
*Salon.* 8 January 2012,
http://www.salon.com/2012/01/08/what_occupy_can_learn_from_the_hunger_games/.

'Fresh Hell'
Laura Miller
*New Yorker.* 14 June 2010,
http://www.newyorker.com/arts/critics/atlarge/2010/06/14/100614crat_atlarge_miller.

# YOU HERE TO FINISH ME OFF, SWEETHEART?

**PEETA MELLARK**
THE HUNGER GAMES

# Fan Appreciation no.1
## V. Arrow on The Panem Companion & more

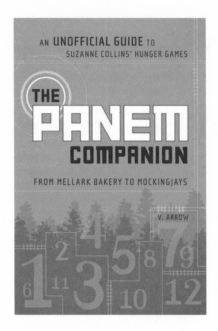

V. Arrow is the foremost commentator and fan academic of The Hunger Games series. She is the author of *The Panem Companion: From Mellark Bakery to Mockingjays* (2012) – an unofficial guide to the series published by Smart Pop Books. She has also authored numerous fanfiction volumes based around The Hunger Games. Arrow graduated from Know College in 2008 with degrees in history and creative writing, specializing in twentieth-century pop culture and young adult lit. She has spoken as an expert on The Hunger Games at San Diego Comic-Con 2013, GeekGirlCon 2012 and the Northern Arizona University School of Social Behaviors '*Hunger Games: Catching Fire*' *Conference* (18 November 2013).

**Nicola Balkind (NB):** When did you first pick up The Hunger Games (THG) books, and what drew you to the series?

**V. Arrow (VA):** I was actually pretty late to the Hunger Games … game, haha. I didn't read the books until just after *Mockingjay* came out because I'd heard that the cliffhanger endings of the previous two were killer, and I'm frankly terrible with suspense! I'm also wary of a lot of sci-fi and dystopian/post-apocalyptic books, because I have a lower capacity to willingly suspend disbelief and like to have a thorough grounding in a series through its world-building. The Hunger Games promises on all fronts, though, as far as I'm concerned, so I'm glad that I did finally get over my fear of cliffhanger endings and read them!

**NB:** What was it that you recognized as unique about THG early on?

**VA:** Well, as I said, I'm terrible with willingly suspending disbelief in alternate-Earth settings: if it's post-apocalyptic, I want to know what the apocalypse was and I want to clearly see those effects in the world that's risen from the old; if there is fantastical technology, I want to see how it would be possible in being borne from modern science; if there is an evil regime, I need to be able to discern what its party politics would be and how they could have been able to wrest control and convince the public of their 'goodness' in the first place. The Hunger Games is very unique because it honestly doesn't really answer any of those questions, but gives just enough information through Katniss's narrow lens as a protagonist about what her world is *to her* that I don't mind not having particulars. The way that Collins wrote Katniss's point of view is brilliant, in my opinion, because she actually comes across as what she is – an oppressed, depressed, teenage girl who is deeply entrenched in her culture and very focused on her personal situation and needs, and a girl who was educated in an extremely propagandist and reductionist school system – than as an author trying to convince us of 'what Katniss is'. I've seen people complain about the series having been written in first person, but I don't think THG would have the impact that it does if it had been written any other way.

**NB:** How did you first come to be involved in the Panem-verse/Hunger Games fandom?

**VA:** Honestly? My favourite characters are Finnick, Annie and Cinna, and one of my friends and I were chatting and we thought we wanted to know more about District 4. It ended up being a marathon mapmaking session until about five in the morning, fuelled mainly by ice cream, and I just posted it to my LiveJournal for fun. That's the map that ended up in *Entertainment Weekly* and got me a book deal, though, so it was the most productive middle-of-the-night ice-cream-and-gigglefest of my life! (So far …)

I've also always been heavily involved in fandom. Making things, transformative works, is the primary way that I interact with media, and that's part of why I moved into working with pop culture analysis and criticism (and literary criticism) – I internalize things very deeply, and it's important to me that the things that I'm taking in, and therefore putting out, are well-considered and purposeful and don't harm people in their executions. When we were making our Panem map, even though it was just in fun for ourselves, I really wanted to make sure that it took actual text and subtext and context from the novels into account and reflected something plausible that made Katniss's world an actual rich, developed world, the way that we get glimpses of on the Victory Tour in *Catching Fire*. I think if you love something, then (1) it's not hard to put a lot of time, thought and effort into it, and (2) it's fun to do that, so why not?

**NB:** What do you think it is about The Hunger Games that brings people together?

**VA:** I think on the one hand, anything that has a huge surge of vocal fans begets more fans because it's human nature to want to share experiences. It's why people prefer seeing sports played live to watching them on TV, and it's why people share their favourite music and TV shows with their friends, and it's why books that have a large reception – like The Hunger Games, Twilight (Stephenie Meyer, 2005-2008), Harry Potter (J.K. Rowling, 1997-2007), The Fault in Our Stars (John Green, 2012), The Da Vinci Code (Dan Brown, 2003), even 50 Shades of Grey (E. L. James, 2011) – seem to dominate the literary/pop culture landscape for such a long time after they come out: people want to like stuff and want to like it together. And to that end, I think that's another thing that makes The Hunger Games special … it's partially about that phenomenon. The Hunger Games is a hugely popular media sensation not only in our world, but its own, and I think that the meta and the irony of that helps propel it in our own consciousness. You can't help getting caught up in the action … and then wondering which character it makes you most like that you're caught up in the action!

The Hunger Games is as much a story about our own world as it is about Panem, because, of course, our world is what enables Panem to happen, and I think people are very invested in trying to figure out how and why.

**NB:** Do you have any experiences with in-person Hunger Games meet-ups?

**VA:** Not really, unfortunately! I did give a panel on race and gender in Panem at the Seattle comic conference, GeekGirlCon 2012, but I didn't really get a chance to meet up with anyone! The panel ran long and it was a little chaotic leaving the hall. Since then I've spoken at San Diego Comic-Con 2013 and I was the keynote speaker at the Northern Arizona University School of Social Behaviors *'Hunger Games: Catching Fire' Conference*.

**NB:** In your experience, have Hunger Games fans been mostly readers or people who are new to reading?

**VA:** Ooh, that's a tough question. The fans I've interacted with have mainly been big readers, but some of my students (in my day job) who are not fans of reading still read and enjoyed THG. I think it's probably a fairly even split?

**NB:** Is the fandom predominantly female or is it more balanced?

**VA:** I think that like most book fandoms, it skews heavily female – since there's a documented problem with attracting boys to reading, especially reading YA [young adult] books – but I have noticed a larger male presence, for sure, in THG fandom than the fandoms for books like Twilight, Divergent (Veronica Roth, 2011-2013), Delirium (Lauren Oliver, 2011-2013), Percy Jackson and the Olympians (Rick Riordan, 2005-2009) or The Fault in Our Stars. I think it's reminiscent of the Harry Potter fandom?

**NB:** In your rereads, have you had any surprising changes in perspective? Anything you loved and grew to dislike or vice versa?

**VA:** Ooh, another good question. I have to admit that like a lot of readers, I missed the intricacies of how Collins illustrated race, on my first reading. Obviously that's changed, and I'm very glad (and I'm a better reader for it, in general!). And obviously things like foreshadowing are much easier to see on a second reading than a first. But I still feel the same way about most of the characters.

**Fan Appreciation no.1**
V. Arrow

**NB:** Favourite book and scene, and why?

**VA:** I love Finnick and Annie's reunion in *Mockingjay*, I love Madge bringing her mother's morphling to the Everdeens' house for Gale's wounds, and I love Mags claiming that her special talent for the Gamemakers will be 'napping'!

**NB:** What is it about a book, series, band or fandom that makes you want to create your own stories around it?

**VA:** Open-endedness. I don't want to write things just for the heck of it; I get most inspired by fandoms that have genuine loose threads or gaps or places to fill a space. Most of my Hunger Games fics were written to explore either characters who aren't as fleshed out in the series or thematic elements that I noticed but was curious to see explored as the major element of a dystopian 'Panem' of their own. And of course, I love the other Districts (besides 12)! I wanted to write about life in those and see if I could feel out their cultures and nuances – even as pretended places in my head – the way that Collins fleshed out Katniss's woods and Hob and home.

**NB:** What are some of the most meaningful responses you've had from other fans? Most discouraging?

**VA:** The most discouraging responses have been the same things that discourage me most about general responses to The Hunger Games: that 'making a big deal' about the role of race and gender in the series is 'overthinking something good and making it not fun'. Not true, and minimalizing of a serious issue! The most meaningful response is honestly getting a response at all. In fandom, it's a complete luck of the draw whether people respond to – or even notice – your work, whether it's good or bad, and I happened to be very lucky with my Hunger Games map and some of my Hunger Games fics.

**NB:** You gained a lot of attention with your map of Panem. Did your map lead to your book deal? Tell me how that came about.

**VA:** Yes, it did! The map actually led to my friend and co-mapmaker, Meg, and me being guests on the first episode of *the Hunger Games Fireside Chat* podcast, hosted by Adam Spunberg and Savanna New [see Fan

Appreciation no. 4], and being subsequent guests on a few episodes sporadically after that. They interviewed my publisher's lead editor, Leah Wilson, about their other Hunger Games book, the anthology *The Girl Who Was On Fire* (2011), and made an introduction after she'd mentioned being interested in my map and I mentioned being interested in writing a lit-crit book about THG. We chatted on the phone about what sort of material I would be interested in writing for a book about The Hunger Games, and she talked to her publishing team. They took a huge chance on me, since Smart Pop Books generally doesn't work with debut writers or 'no names' like me, and I'm very, very grateful that they did.

**NB:** What has been the personal and professional impact of combining your own fandom with writing fanfiction and your own book?

**VA:** I haven't noticed anything too major, really. It's not like a multi-million dollar franchise deal like The Mortal Instruments (Cassandra Clare, 2007-2014) or a scandalous publishing tale like E. L. James's search-and-replace fic-to-book story with 50 Shades. I worked very hard with *The Panem Companion* to make it separate and distinct from my fanfiction and fanworks, even though obviously the map was just a further revision of my original fannish map and the etymology/lexicon is an edited version of what I had posted on my blog back in 2011. And I also work very hard within my fanworks and professional pieces not to put anything out in the world that I can't either stand by (best case scenario) or apologize for and try to learn from (as a worst-case scenario). I assume that the main reason it hasn't affected me much has been that *The Panem Companion* is nonfiction about a fairly benign topic – literary criticism and The Hunger Games – so we'll see whether future endeavours make me feel differently ...

**Fan Appreciation no.1**
V. Arrow

GO FURTHER

Books

*Divergent Thinking: Young Adult Authors on the Divergent Trilogy*
Leah Wilson (ed.)
(Dallas: Smart Pop Books, 2014)

*Fic!: Why Fanfiction is Taking Over the World*
Anne Jamison (ed.)
(Dallas: Smart Pop Books, 2013)

*The Panem Companion: An Unofficial Guide to Suzanne Collins' Hunger Games, From Mellark Bakery to Mockingjays*
V. Arrow
(Dallas: Smart Pop Books, 2012)

*The Girl Who Was on Fire: Your Favorite Authors on Suzanne Collins' Hunger Games Trilogy*
Leah Wilson (ed.)
(Dallas: Smart Pop Books, 2011)

**Online**

*V. Arrow Books*, http://varrowbooks.tumblr.com/
*V. Arrow at Smart Pop Books*, http://www.smartpopbooks.com/authors/v-arrow
*V's Fan Fiction archive*, http://higherarrowsfic.livejournal.com/

# MY REFUSAL TO PLAY THE GAMES ON THE CAPITOL'S TERMS IS TO BE MY LAST ACT OF REBELLION.

**KATNISS EVERDEEN**
CATCHING FIRE

Chapter
3

# The Gender Games: Katniss & The 'Strong Female Character'

→ Hunger Games heroine Katniss Everdeen is a unique female protagonist. In many ways she is perhaps the most strong, stereotypically masculine and atypically gender-defined hero of any recent book or film, particularly in the young adult genre. In this chapter we will look at the success of *The Hunger Games* film which brought Katniss to mainstream prominence and the gender debates that discussions surrounding the film presented.

Fig. 1: Katniss: Beacon of Hope Fan Art.

We'll also take a look at how Katniss is depicted within the series, the extent to which her behaviour can be classed as stereotypically masculine or feminine, and how audiences perceive these differences from the norm.

Please note that for the purposes of this chapter I will be using definitions according to a limited gender binary, as represented in the language of Suzanne Collins. Let us assume that the Capitol's orders for Districts to make Tribute of twelve boys and twelve girls indicates that boys and girls are considered to be members of two distinct biological categories, and therefore social groups, in Panem. Though limiting, 'female' will be defined as cisgender (or 'gender normative') and self-identifying as female or feminine, and 'male' will be defined as cisgender and self-identifying as male or masculine, or any of the above as identified by Katniss in her narration.

*The Hunger Games* movie earned over $690 million at the global box office, and amid its success many essays and web articles sprung up lauding the series as different than its closest predecessor, the Twilight series (Stephenie Meyer, 2005-2008). Twilight has come under scrutiny from many critics who feel that Bella Swan is a weaker, and at times subservient, female character. In contrast, Collins's approach to gender roles has, on the whole, been celebrated for its relative complexity. Let's take the lay of the land.

Currently, the 'strong female character' is having a moment in popular culture. Equally, it is the subject of criticism by many, including Sarah Dunn at *PolicyMic*, who says, 'Enough With the "Strong Female Characters", Already,' and Sophia McDougall who simply wrote, 'I Hate Strong Female Characters.' Natalie Portman has also weighed in, and was quoted by *PolicyMic* as saying:

> The fallacy in Hollywood is that if you're making a "feminist" story, the woman kicks ass and wins. That's not feminist, that's macho. A movie about a weak, vulnerable woman can be feminist if it shows a real person that we can empathize with.

In a recent study entitled 'Violent Female Action Characters in Contemporary American Cinema', academic Katy Gilbatric conducted a content analysis of violent female action characters shown in American action films from 1991 through 2005. The analysis focused on three aspects: gender stereotypes, demographics, and quantity and type of violence. In a section quoted in *Wired*, she writes,

> The [violent female action character] is a recent addition to contemporary American cinema and has the potential to redefine female heroines, for better or worse. This research provides evidence that the majority of female action characters shown in American cinema are not empowering images, they do not draw on their femininity as a source of power, and they are not a kind of 'post woman' operating outside the boundaries of gender restrictions.

The Gender Games: Katniss & The 'Strong Female Character'

According to the abstract, the author's findings 'suggest continued gender stereotypes set within a violent framework of contemporary American cinema'. Taking this as an indication of the climate into which Katniss (as a star movie character) was born, let's take a look at reactions in the media.

*Jezebel*'s Melissa Silverstein commented on the sheer exposure of *The Hunger Games* the day before the movie premiered. Over 2,000 screens were sold out ahead of opening weekend, and the writer points out that the film was due to open on approximately 4,000 screens, while *Twilight: Breaking Dawn* Part 2 (Bill Condon, 2012, the fifth movie instalment in the saga) opened in a mere 62 screens more. (She also gives credit to Twilight for 'setting the table' for *The Hunger Games*.) Silverstein argues both sides: why it's good that little attention was focused on the film's female protagonist as a point of importance; and why, at the same time, it is remarkable. She observes that the romance element of the story was not focused upon until the final week of marketing, stating that, 'I'm sure it is a testament to the book, but it is also a testament to the diversity of fans.' On the negative side, however, she writes that

> at the same time it DOES matter that Katniss is a girl and people – men, women, boys and girls – are all interested in seeing this film. This has the potential to show Hollywood where honestly it is already a hit even before it opens and finding the next potential franchise is on everyone's mind, that having a strong female character is not something to try and avoid, it is something to be seen as a potential success.

While female-led franchises are often seen as box office poison, or follow a hypersexualized, violent female protagonist dressed in masculine qualities and tight clothing (think *Catwoman* [Pitof, 2004], *Salt* [Phillip Noyce, 2010] and *Aeon Flux* [Karyn Kusama, 2005]), Katniss, on the other hand, is not sexualized – which we'll come back to in detail in a moment. Despite this, Jennifer Lawrence still came under media scrutiny; more specifically, her looks did. In her review of *The Hunger Games*, *New York Times* film critic Manohla Dargis wrote, 'A few years ago Ms. Lawrence might have looked hungry enough to play Katniss, but now, at 21, her seductive, womanly figure makes a bad fit for a dystopian fantasy about a people starved into submission.' Many more comments were made in the media about Lawrence's size and height relative to her co-star and Katniss's male love interest, Peeta, played by Josh Hutcherson. *Slate*'s L. V. Anderson was quick to respond, asking, 'why haven't they been more consistent in their critiques of actors' bodies? [...] I haven't seen much concern about Liam Hemsworth's muscular frame, even though his character in *The Hunger Games* occupies the same food-strapped world as Katniss.' Further, she argues,

> Movie critics suspend their disbelief all the time – and when they suddenly refuse to do so for a female actor whose body looks more like an average woman's body rather

*Fig. 2: Katniss and Peeta in the Training Centre.*

than less, it's hard to see that as anything but sexist.

Misogyny in the media seems inevitable, and this charge demonstrates a real-world hang-up on the physical portrayal of femininity. This leads us to Suzanne Collins's own handling of masculinity and femininity in The Hunger Games. Every well-rounded character in fiction is likely to embody some traits from each gender (as they are typically understood and stereotyped). Katniss is particularly interesting because not only does she demonstrate both masculine and feminine traits, but the scales tip in favour of the more masculine. In 'Katniss and the Politics of Gender', Jessica Miller outlines Katniss's leaning towards masculine traits thus:

> Bucking the popular culture trend of the helpless girlfriend who needs to be saved by her man, Collins presents Katniss as the strong one. Yet Katniss still needs Peeta's warmth and decency. Even their postwar domestic life bucks gender expectations: Peeta begs for children and Katniss relents; Peeta bakes and Katniss hunts. The romance between Katniss and Peeta offers a welcome foil to the many romances in popular culture that hew closely to the expectations of stereotypical femininity and masculinity.

Kelsey Wallace of *bitchmagazine.org* takes this further, delving into the relative femininity of Peeta's primary characteristics in direct opposition with Katniss's more masculine ones. While Gale, as the third point of the triangle, is conventionally masculine and, as Wallace puts it, 'follows the "masculine" logic that men form bonds through shared activity as opposed to shared feelings (the woman's way of bonding™)', Peeta, on the other hand,

> possesses many traits we associate with femininity – he's artistic, he's intuitive, he cries in front of people, he wears his heart on his sleeve – he's emotionally vulnerable in a way we don't think of heroes as being emotionally vulnerable. Pretty and sensitive.

A few weeks after Dargis's review in which she concerned herself with Lawrence's appearance as Katniss, she took part in a discussion with colleague A. O. Scott in a piece entitled 'A Radical Female Hero from Dystopia'. Here, Dargis questions our stereotypical ideas of what is masculine and what is feminine thus:

> I mean, is killing masculine? Is nurturing feminine? Katniss nurtures and she kills, and she does both extremely well. Katniss is a fantasy figure, but partly what makes her powerful – and, I suspect, what makes her so important to a lot of girls and women – is that she's one of the truest feeling, most complex female characters to hit American movies in a while. She isn't passive, she isn't weak, and she isn't some random girl. She's active, she's strong and she's the girl who motivates the story.

This type of action, as mentioned above, typifies the hyper-sexualized violent female hero. So what is it that sets Katniss apart from other heroines, and why does she succeed with audiences? Blogger Caroline Heldman wrote:

> Katniss succeeds with audiences where other women heroes have failed because she isn't an FFT. Fighting fuck toys are hyper-sexualized women protagonists who are able to 'kick ass' (and kill) with the best of them – and look good doing it. The FFT appears empowered, but her very existence serves the pleasure of the heterosexual male viewer. In short, the FFT takes female agency and appropriates it for the male gaze.

Heldman also notes that box office flops like *Catwoman* (Pitof, 2004) and *Sucker Punch* (Zack Snyder, 2011) have, in the past, led movie production companies to conclude that women leads aren't bankable – but the problem is that they were portrayed as objects or FFTs rather than subjects. Whether you are on the side of Bella Swan – a character whose compunction towards troubling gender stereotypes is well documented – or not, one could argue that she is still a rounded, 'subject' character. Heldman's is a simple point, but one that goes a long way to explain the ongoing success of Katniss Everdeen and The Hunger Games franchise. Fans also weigh in on this topic, pitting Katniss and The Hunger Games against Twilight. As *Slate*'s Ben Blatt points out, 'Of the tens of millions

*Fig. 3: Finnick uses his sexu-
ality to intimidate Katniss.*

who identify themselves on Facebook as fans of either of the two series, less than 20 percent are fans of both.' As the books were released, an intense debate began within the fandom. While some mirrored Twilight's Team Edward/Team Jacob dynamic, fans of The Hunger Games did something different. Rather than camping with Team Gale or Team Peeta, many shirked the love triangle set-up in favour of a third option: Team Katniss.

The interplay between Katniss's gender and her masculine traits is also explored throughout the books. While preparing for her Hunger Games interview debut, Katniss notes that female Tributes are usually touted as scary or sexy. Haymitch trains her, telling her to try to act humble, cocky, mysterious – to no avail. Eventually he gives up and Cinna tells her to imagine she's only talking to him instead, but as she twirls in the dress he designed for her, she is at her most feminine. Katniss also defines her own femininity and strengths in opposition to those of her mother and sister: Katniss is healing as well as nurturing – as Peeta points out in the cave as she nurses him back to health – but she rejects this notion. Her sexuality is also at play in the cave: as she describes her playful kisses she says she is imitating her mother and father, aware that she has, until this point, withdrawn from sexual attention. In *Catching Fire*, the Victor elite tease Katniss for her asexuality: Finnick offers her a sugar cube and makes suggestive comments, Johanna strips naked in front of her, and Chaff plants a kiss on her lips. Peeta catches on while Katniss is shaken by their forthrightness.

Anita Sarkeesian, who publishes at *Feminist Frequency*, also applauds both Suzanne Collins's and the film-makers' decision not to reduce Katniss to her gender or sexualize

The Gender Games: Katniss & The 'Strong Female Character'

Fig. 4: Finnick and Annie's
relationship is explored in
a webseries by Mainstay
Productions.

her in either the books or *The Hunger Games* film. In her series of videos on The Hunger Games, Sarkeesian states that the way Katniss deals with violence is unique, especially when compared with other so-called strong female characters (e.g. The Bride in *Kill Bill* [Quentin Tarantino, 2003], Hit Girl in *Kick-Ass* [Matthew Vaughn, 2010]). Katniss is not completely desensitized, and a key indicator is the way she mourns Rue's death. This and the representation of Katniss's PTSD, Sarkeesian stated, were refreshing, and – importantly, in terms of Katniss as a subject character – these vulnerabilities make her a stronger character rather than a weaker one.

Alyssa Rosenberg at *Think Progress* makes a similar point about Katniss in the context of female action heroes and the American tradition. Katniss handles Rue's death in a way that at first conforms with the kick-ass heroine stereotype as she shoots Rue's killer in immediate revenge, then turns it on its head by laying Rue to rest, crying emphatically. Rosenberg writes, 'The scene was striking because it's so contrary to the way we've tended to frame female action heroines in recent years. They handle acts of violence calmly.' At times Katniss does handle violence calmly, but only when the violent act is performed to save her own life, and these actions are not without tumultuous consequences.

The way in which Katniss responds to violence is perfectly encapsulated in her character during peaceful times doing what she loves: to hunt. In an article that compared Katniss with real-life young huntresses, CNN's *Eatocracy* contributor Sarah Letrent writes,

'Katniss is a good representation of female hunters. We're not what you expect,' Mikayla says. 'We can be pretty just like any other girl, even if we're not afraid to get dirty.' Fifteen-year-old Savannah Rogers of Cleveland, Georgia, also grew up hunting and pored through the 'Hunger Games' trilogy. 'Katniss is a very independent young woman like me, who enjoys the outdoor environment. We both like the peace and tranquility offered by the cover of the trees,' she says. 'Hunting offers an escape for the both of us so that we can forget our troubling lives outside of our territory.'

Beyond Katniss's territory comes confrontation with the emotional ideals of gender and sex, and her most headstrong masculine personality traits butt up against societal expectations. In terms of a masculine–feminine binary, Katniss as a character is often criticized for her stoicism. In 'Will the Real Katniss Everdeen Please Stand Up?' *Victor's Village* contributor Satsuma writes:

Unfortunately, Katniss not being a stereotypical female in some (though NOT all) respects, has led to her being harshly judged by many fans for not following the Stand By Your Man routine when Peeta's hijacked. She's also judged for not forgiving Gale for his part in Prim's death. Because, of course, women are all supposed to be unconditionally loving, forgiving, and Emotionally Supportive, as opposed to those stone-faced males who have the emotional capacity of a teaspoon.

Throughout the books, Katniss appears unemotional at times. She is often disconnected from emotional triggers or is actively screening herself from painful thoughts and situations. This runs counter to Peeta's relative vulnerability and Gale's emotionally charged (read: angry) rants against the Capitol. While Katniss's stereotypically masculine solemnity is derided by many, Peeta's more feminine sensitivity often goes without comment. This reversal of traditional gender roles confronts many of our preconceptions about gender and, by doing something unusual, creates conflict within the story and brings out a great deal of debate in the real world.

Katniss is a tomboy, and her masculine traits often act as a protective barrier against the world. What she must come to terms with are her feminine traits, which are presented as a double threat as she navigates the feminine sides of both her personality and her physical appearance under public gaze. As Peeta and Gale discuss in *Mockingjay*, Katniss will choose a partner based on her best chance of survival, rather than for love, which also hardens audiences' perceptions of her. In contrast to Katniss, Finnick is a strong, handsome character with deep sensitivity like Peeta. He is presented in a way that is unlike other male characters: for example, he is a prostitute for the Capitol, an unusual storyline for a male. His love story is also set in opposition to Katniss and Peeta's: while the star-crossed lovers' story is filled with artifice, Finnick and Annie's enduring love is rewarded with a wedding free of Capitol contrivance. While the majority of love and marriage stories focus on the bride, Finnick is front and centre. Meanwhile his wife-to-be is shown as a highly vulnerable, very feminine character, as sweet and helpless as Prim was at the beginning of *The Hunger Games*. Despite having won the Games herself, Annie is ruined by the experience and her mentor Mags, like Katniss, volunteers in Annie's place.

Katniss is also wary of being portrayed as physically feminine, and much of this is tied up in the performative aspect of the Hunger Games, from being selected to how she thinks she'll be portrayed on-screen in the Arena. For example, she keeps herself from crying at the Reaping so as not to appear as an easy target. During her Capitol makeover, she describes the action as though it is happening outside of herself, like she is not an active agent in the beautification of her face and body. During the Hunger Games interview process she demonstrates a flourish of femininity, as mentioned above, but it does not last. This interplay between her mental and physically masculine traits comes to a head at the end of this process: when Peeta announces his love for her, she argues that he has made her look weak; Haymitch counters that Peeta made her desirable. These moments, much as she hates them, allow Katniss to draw power from her feminine traits and are most instrumental in her growth as a character.

As Collins and the film-makers are breaking the binds of traditional gender roles, Katniss also takes on roles beyond her gender which she must learn to navigate. These go beyond the Capitol's punishment in all its forms (poverty, imprisonment, compulsory fights to the death, and even physical beautification), and into the murky arena of identity. A.O. Scott places Katniss' many identities both in terms of the story and the larger cultural context thus:

> as she sprints through the forest, Katniss is carrying the burden of multiple symbolic identities. She's an athlete, a media celebrity and a warrior as well as a sister, a daughter, a loyal friend and (potential) girlfriend. In genre terms she is a western hero, an action hero, a romantic heroine and a tween idol [...] and also the synthesis of Harry Potter and Bella Swan – the Boy Who Lived and the Girl Who Must Choose. Ms. Collins's novels are able to fuse all of these meanings into a credible character embedded in an exciting and complex story.

Believing in Katniss is a major element in the story; it's what makes us empathize and root for Panem at large. In 'Will the Real Katniss Everdeen Please Stand Up?' *Victor's Village* contributor Satsuma also addresses the issue of Katniss's identity – or, rather, identities, all of which she must embody to ignite the fight against the Capitol:

> And much like the overall story offers different things to different people, so does its heroine, Katniss Everdeen. Marshall Bruce Mathers III created not just one persona, 'Eminem', but also the 'Slim Shady' persona as a spinoff of that. Well, Katniss, along the course of the story, also acquires several different personas. The Girl on Fire. The Star-Crossed Lover. The Mockingjay.

Before the Games, Katniss's life relied on activities directly correlating with subsistence: hunting, trading, taking care of Prim, and so on. Not only is her day-to-day life redefined by action, but personas and identities are bestowed upon her. The Girl on Fire and the Star-Crossed Lover from District 12 go hand-in-hand, but are also opposing identities. When she behaves in the mould of one identity at the expense of another, it creates opportunities for ridicule, making her life a constant compromise between personas and identities. This includes fluctuations in the distribution of her masculine and feminine characteristics, the reactions to which are not limited to the storyworld, but also take place in the public discourse.

Katniss is certainly a character who reaches beyond this faux feminist, 'strong female character' Hollywood fad. Her masculine traits are not simply active and violent, they are coping mechanisms, instincts to protect and survive. When she breaks emotionally, it is not with irrationality or loss of control, but with empathy, believability and grace. It is without sexualization, with flaws and with multifaceted gendered traits that Katniss becomes the 'strong female character' who stands out against Hollywood's army of female action characters which fail to empower. She is The Girl on Fire, the Mockingjay, and the leader of a revolution. ●

## GO FURTHER

### Extracts/Articles/Essays

'"She Has No Idea The Effect She Can Have": Katniss and the Politics of Gender'
Jessica Miller
In *The Hunger Games and Philosophy: A Critique of Pure Treason* (2012)
George A. Dunn and Nicholas Michaud (eds)
(New Jersey: John Wiley & Sons, 2012)
[Quoted in *bitchmedia*: http://bitchmagazine.org/post/the-rebel-warrior-and-the-boy-with-the-bread-gale-peeta-and-masculinity-in-the-hunger-games]

'Violent Female Action Characters in Contemporary American Cinema'
Katy Gilpatric
In *Sex Roles*. 62. 11–12 (2010), pp 734–46 [Online], http://link.springer.com/article/10.100 7%2Fs11199-010-9757-7 [Quoted in *Wired*: http://www.wired.com/underwire/2012/03/ katniss-everdeen-hollywood-heroines/2/].

### Film

*Catwoman*, Pitof, dir. (USA: Warner Bros., 2004).
*Twilight: Breaking Dawn – Part 2*, Bill Condon, dir. (USA: Summit Entertainment, 2012).
*Sucker Punch*, Zack Snyder, dir. (USA: Warner Bros., 2011).
*Kick-Ass*, Matthew Vaughn, dir. (UK: Marv Films, 2010).
*Salt*, Phillip Noyce, dir. (USA: Columbia Pictures, 2010).
*Twilight*, Catherine Hardwicke, dir. (USA: Summit Entertainment, 2008).
*Kill Bill: Vol. 1*, Quentin Tarantino, dir. (USA: Miramax Films, 2003).

### Online

'A Textual Analysis of The Hunger Games'
Ben Blatt
*Slate*. 20 November 2013,
http://www.slate.com/articles/arts/culturebox/2013/11/hunger_games_catching_ fire_a_textual_analysis_of_suzanne_collins_novels.html.

'Enough With the "Strong Female Characters", Already'
Sarah Dunn
*PolicyMic*. 9 October 2013,
http://www.policymic.com/articles/66469/enough-with-the-strong-female-characters-already.

48

The Gender Games: Katniss & The 'Strong Female Character'

'I Hate Strong Female Characters'
Sophia McDougall
*New Statesman.* 15 August 2013,
http://www.newstatesman.com/culture/2013/08/i-hate-strong-female-characters.

'Will the Real Katniss Everdeen Please Stand Up?'
Satsuma
*Victor's Village.* 11 December 2012,
http://victorsvillage.com/2012/12/11/will-the-real-katniss-everdeen-please-stand-up-part-1/.

'The Hunger Games Movie vs. the Book (Part II)'
Anita Sarkeesian
*Feminist Frequency.* 12 April 2012, http://www.feministfrequency.com/2012/04/the-hunger-game-a-book-and-movie-comparison/.

'The Hunger Games Novel & Katniss Everdeen (Part I)'
Anita Sarkeesian
*Feminist Frequency.* 10 April 2012,
http://www.feministfrequency.com/2012/04/the-hunger-games-katniss-part-1-the-novel/.

'A Radical Female Hero from Dystopia'
A. O. Scott and Manohla Dargis
*New York Times.* 8 April 2012,
http://www.nytimes.com/2012/04/08/movies/katniss-everdeen-a-new-type-of-woman-warrior.html?_r=1&pagewanted=all?src=tp.

'The Hunger Games, Hollywood and Fighting Fuck Toys'
Caroline Heldman
*Ms. Magazine Blog.* 5 April 2012,
http://msmagazine.com/blog/2012/04/06/the-hunger-games-hollywood-and-fighting-fuck-toys/.

'Katniss Everdeen, Female Action Heroes, and the American Tradition'
Alyssa Rosenberg
*Think Progress.* 5 April 2012,
http://thinkprogress.org/alyssa/2012/04/05/458589/katniss-everdeen-female-action-heroes-and-the-american-tradition/.

'Jennifer Lawrence Is Not "Too Big" To Play Katniss'
L. V. Anderson
*Slate*. 23 March 2012,
http://www.slate.com/blogs/browbeat/2012/03/23/jennifer_lawrence_s_body_not_
skinny_enough_to_play_katniss_.html.

'The Rebel Warrior and the Boy with the Bread: Gale, Peeta, and Masculinity in the Hunger Games'
Kelsey Wallace
*bitchmedia*. 6 March 2012,
http://bitchmagazine.org/post/the-rebel-warrior-and-the-boy-with-the-bread-gale-
peeta-and-masculinity-in-the-hunger-games

'Will The Hunger Games Be The First Real Female Franchise?'
Melissa Silverstein
*Jezebel*. 22 March 2012,
http://jezebel.com/5895544/will-the-hunger-games-be-the-first-real-female-fran-
chise.

'Tested by a Picturesque Dystopia'
Manohla Dargis
*New York Times*. 22 March 2012,
http://www.nytimes.com/2012/03/23/movies/the-hunger-games-movie-adapts-the-
suzanne-collins-novel.html.

'The Hunger Games bucks hunter stereotypes'
Sarah Letrent
*Eatocracy*. 16 March 2012,
http://eatocracy.cnn.com/2012/03/16/the-hunger-games-bucks-hunter-
stereotypes/?hpt=hp_bn12.

'Gender Roles in the Series'
Dragonclaws (pseud.)
*Fanpop Hunger Games Forum* [n.d.]. http://www.fanpop.com/clubs/the-hunger-
games/articles/159399/title/gender-roles-series.

# Chapter
# 4

# Propos:
# The Publicity vs
# The Message

→ **Suzanne Collins's The Hunger Games contains some deeply pertinent and political messages about the nature of war, poverty, and the dangers of reality television and celebrity culture. As we touched upon in Chapter 2: 'Hunger for the Games: War & Violence', Lionsgate's marketing of the movies takes a transmedia storytelling approach in which many of the key themes play out as if in-universe.**

The marketing for *The Hunger Games* movie was all about the Arena; the marketing for *Catching Fire* is all about celebrity – Katniss, Peeta and the Victors entering the Quarter Quell as pre-made Capitol idols; and, at the time of writing, marketing for *Mockingjay* is yet to come. Let's look at each of these in turn.

### Withholding the Hunger Games

The Hunger Games book series became one of the most challenged texts for the American Library Association (ALA) in 2011. The organization counted 326 reported attempts to restrict or remove books from schools and libraries in 2011, giving all three books the top three positions on the list, with complaints like 'anti-ethnic; anti-family; insensitivity; offensive language; occult/satanic; violence'. There is no doubt that the series contains dark themes and scenes of violence, as evidenced by *The Hunger Games* film earning a PG-13 rating in the United States and a 12A in the United Kingdom. The MPAA rated the film PG-13 for 'intense sequences of violence and action, some frightening images, thematic elements, a suggestive situation and language'. In the United Kingdom, Lionsgate received advice from the British Board of Film Classification (BBFC) to cut 7 seconds of footage to secure the rating, which they opted for over the uncut '15' certificate version, which was also available. The BBFC insight notes read as follows: 'Contains intense threat, moderate violence and occasional gory moments.' With a 12A rating the publicity for the film, therefore, would reach its target demographic before the watershed in daytime TV spots, online marketing, and through merchandizing opportunities.

In a piece for *Slate*, Katie Roiphe investigated the marketing philosophy behind the first movie, asking 'Is *The Hunger Games* Publicity Too Hunger Games-ish?' She quotes Tim Palen, head marketeer for Lionsgate, who stated that, 'We made a rule that we would never say "23 kids get killed." We say "only one wins."' Roiphe compares this with Orwellian doublespeak which 'pussyfoots' around the very point of the novel: brutality. To their credit (from a fan's perspective), Lionsgate led with a campaign which showed no footage at all from the Games – a bid which may have been motivated to save the money shot, appease and excite existing fans of the books, or play it safe. However, as the *LA Times* reported, a back-up plan was in place. Ben Fritz writes: 'If the movie was not generating sufficient interest, new ads would have been cut to show more of the gladiatorial action. (A spokesman for the studio declined to make Palen available for an interview.)'

This is where the conflict between the marketing and Suzanne Collins's message truly begins. Each time Collins invokes violence, her words serve to condemn violent actions. By withholding violence from the film trailer, audiences are not cajoled by scenes of gladiatorial victory. However, if this plan had gone ahead – and indeed it did in small part through the 'one wins' versus '23 get killed' framing – this spin on the story serves to foreground victory. While this may intrigue audiences, the approach also

*Fig. 1: The Victory Tour poster.*

VICTORY TOUR
WITH KATNISS EVERDEEN AND PEETA MELLARK
WINNERS OF THE 74ᵗʰ HUNGER GAMES

mimics the message of the Capitol, whose annual Hunger Games propaganda concludes with the following message, which is hinted at in the book and delivered in full during *The Hunger Games* film:

> And so it was decreed, that each year, the various districts of Panem would offer up in tribute, one young man and woman, to fight to the death in a pageant of honour, courage and sacrifice. The lone victor, bathed in riches, would serve as a reminder of our generosity and our forgiveness. This is how we remember our past. This is how we safeguard our future.

Taking some specific marketing techniques from the first movie as examples, Roiphe outlines these key messages from the novel, saying that

> one feels that the great publicity apparatus surrounding the movie, the iPhone game, 'Girl On Fire,' the elaborate spread of costumes in People, which tells you how to get the look of the Capitol, the joyous, frenzied consumption of exploitation, the decadent cultural frothiness of the People package, are precisely what Collins is so eloquently critiquing or describing.

In terms of Lionsgate's marketing butting up against Collins's message, Roiphe hadn't seen nothin' yet.

### The marketing of *Catching Fire*: Life in the Capitol

As the marketing machine switched gears and began to tease the audience ahead of the first *Catching Fire* trailer, the studio released Victory Tour posters: stills from Katniss and Peeta's first outing in the Districts after their Hunger Games victory. These became the skin for the official Facebook and Twitter channels and were marketed across fansites and movie news outlets. In a review of the posters, movie website */Film* (slashfilm.com) called the posters 'sleek, striking, and different enough [...] to be attention-grabbing'. Cracks in the veneer begin to show as the author, Angie Han, adds:

> I also love Lionsgate's strategy of treating us, the viewers, like the citizens of Panem watching at home. The strategy comes with some disturbing implications, since most of the Games audience is either infuriatingly oblivious or desperately impoverished, but it's a neat way of working in the film's themes.

The brunt of the *Catching Fire* transmedia marketing elements kicked off around February 2013. Lionsgate is masterful at the art of the long game when it comes to building hype for its films, particularly online. This layer of transmedia marketing included the launch of *Capitol Couture*, a website that mimics the Capitol in style and tone and focuses on Capitol fashion, lifestyle and even food and drink. The site takes real life designers and places them in-universe as stylists, much like the character Cinna. Lionsgate has since followed this up with some huge merchandizing sales, including a line of clothing in partnership with online fashion retailer Net-a-Porter and a District-inspired make-up line from CoverGirl. Like Suzanne Collins's comments about the nature of news and reality television blurring the lines between what is real and what is fake, these transmedia marketing devices toe the line between bottom-line sales and a murky message about capitalism. To what extent is Lionsgate playing with the form? Are they losing sight of the author's intended message?

Many of the fans I've spoken to about Lionsgate's marketing, including those interviewed in this book, have expressed concern about the direction of the movie media. A representative answer came from Savanna New, co-host of the *Hunger Games Fireside Chat* podcast. When I asked her about the latest developments, specifically *Capitol Couture*, it seemed there was a distinct line that Lionsgate has crossed. She summed up her thoughts thus:

> I think that the Capitol Couture website is great and I even thought the nail polishes they did last year were cool. The CoverGirl Capitol make-up line is neat but I think that the marketing is a bit extreme. The commercials kind of freak me out because they're so Capitol it's just not even funny. You watch the commercial and you're like, where am I? […] Everyone knows that they're doing this to remind us that we are the Capitol, the consumers, but I think it gets to the point where it's unnecessary and it really does contradict Suzanne Collins' message that runs throughout the series.

New also hit upon an alienating factor for the audience of the movies. While Lionsgate termed *The Hunger Games* as a 'four quadrant' film (meaning it appeals to all four key demographics: male, female, over and under 25 years old) these marketing techniques tell a different story. 'They centre so much of the marketing around the fashion and cosmetics that I feel like it leaves out such a huge portion of the fan base,' said New. 'Not every woman is interested in fashion and cosmetics, most men are not, so it's like, Adam, what's in there for you in the marketing for this film?'

Adam Spunberg, New's co-host, responded that he is alienated in that respect, but takes a practical outlook, stating that,

> People can get caught up in the themes of what it represents; I think they [Lionsgate] just realized that selling Capitol-based stuff is more expensive and glitzy and people

Propos: The Publicity vs The Message

will buy it. I don't think it's really a wonderful thing to be doing, considering what the movie franchise is all about, but at the same time I don't blame them for doing it.

Emily Asher-Perrin, a contributor to the science fiction and fantasy website *Tor.com*, wrote a detailed commentary on the *Capitol Couture* website which outlines a number of the same concerns. She writes, 'It's frighteningly real, which is why it's jarring; if the Hunger Games were an activity that the world participated in, it wouldn't be hard to imagine real ads and websites just like the ones being created for *Catching Fire*.' She is of the opinion that Lionsgate's decision to ask real fashion designers to contribute to the project is 'inspired' and lends credibility to the project as a whole.

However, the Capitol Couture website is a test for those trying to find the line between reality and fiction. Within the profile article about Johanna Mason, actual designer Jan Taminiau gives this quote: 'I love creating a fantasy around a woman's body,' a reference to the tree-like garb he has her swathed in. Is this a true comment from the designer about the process of creating her look for the photoshoots and film, or something slipped in there by the author of the fake article to give the piece authenticity? Isn't the point that we can't really tell?

This harkens back to Collins's concerns when flipping between news coverage of the war in Iraq and reality television, this blurring of the line between truth and fiction. Asher-Perrin concludes with a question: 'How could anyone possibly feel good about shopping the Capitol Couture line? What are we saying if we buy these clothes – aren't we buying into the very thing that Suzanne Collins' books are trying to warn us against?'

As Spunberg noted, perhaps we ought to expect a bottom line approach from a huge studio such as Lionsgate; however, their approach has created consternation amongst many members of its core fan base. The extent to which fans are playing make-believe with the Capitol, and the extent to which they are becoming it, are constantly in flux, and Lionsgate is not taking an editorial approach on where those boundaries lie. Tim Palen told *Variety* that, 'There was always a strong sense we should keep (the campaign) authentic and not overtly gross.' However it seems that their purview has overlooked key fan demographics. New also suggested that fans whose interests lie in the Districts rather than the Capitol, may feel alienated, and so might those on lower incomes. As The Girl With The Pearl, a contributor to fansite *Victor's Village*, writes (original emphasis):

By presenting us with what will probably be a luxury (aka 'too expensive for your average gal') fashion line, it feels like Lionsgate is saying that they really don't care what they're selling or what the message of the story really is, as long as we CONSUME. Because the more of us they convince that we are the Capitol – whom we remind you are the ignorant, counter-productive follow-

*Fig. 2: CoverGirl's look for District 11.*

*Fig. 3: Mockingjay.net writers show their disdain for* The Hunger Games *theme park.*

ers of a corrupt society – the more we buy into their bottom line. They're not selling the movie or its message to us. They're just selling. We're curious to see what the fashion line will look like [...] We may even want to buy some but [...] again, we can't. Both because we're poor and because it just feels wrong.

*Celebuzz* posted a far more aloof and irreverent take on the argument via its critique of the CoverGirl make-up line. In a 2013 article entitled 'CoverGirl Helps You Get the Hunger Games Look By Draping You In Weird Feathers, Bits of Twine', Robert Kessler writes: 'There is a look for each district and a tutorial for whichever suits your fancy. Would you rather look like a futuristic stonemason under an oppressive regime or a glam sweatshop worker? With CoverGirl cosmetics, you don't have to choose ...' The author riffs on a few different District looks, concluding with a distancing remark: 'Great troll, CoverGirl. Very funny prank you're playing on all of us.'

As the fervour regarding the make-up looks died down, however, The Hunger Games franchise was making another big splash. Three weeks before the *Catching Fire* release date, fans were up in arms at the news of another possibility: that of a Hunger Games theme park. The initial report from the *Hollywood Reporter* stated that Lionsgate CEO Jon Feltheimer had been, 'approached in two different territories about potential theme park opportunities, which gives you a sense of the cultural impact of this franchise' and that Lionsgate are 'excited about those opportunities and are pursuing them'. Although *The Stir*, the entertainment blog at *cafemom.com*, was quick to post '5 Reasons a "Hunger Games" Theme Park Would Rock Our World', the fans felt differently. As news broke, fans took to Twitter to express their dismay. In an early news story, Hunger Games beat reporter Sara Gruen questioned whether Lionsgate cares what the franchise means to fans, contending that 'a Hunger Games theme park could seriously disenchant their core fanbase', and that, 'The very idea of a theme park based on The Hunger Games flies in the face of everything the series stands for.'

The idea of a Hunger Games theme park also chimes with the Capitol's idea of fun. From *The Hunger Games* book:

The arenas are historic sites, preserved after the Games. Popular destinations for Capitol residents to visit, to vacation. Go for a month, rewatch the Games, tour the catacombs, visit the sites where the deaths took place. You can even take part in reenactments. They say the food is excellent.

Uh oh. In the *Atlantic Wire*, Esther Zuckerman added,

We should not want to emulate Panem in any way. We shouldn't want to dress like

Propos: The Publicity vs The Message

members of the Capitol and we shouldn't want to visit a theme park that immerses us in this world. It's understandable that Lionsgate would want to do as much as possible to make people go see this movie and continue to milk it for all it's worth with a theme park, but perhaps everyone should consider what they are selling.

Still others theorized about what a Hunger Games theme park might entail. An admin on the fansite *Mockingjay.net* wrote:

From what we've seen online so far, Hunger Games fans are completely horrified at this idea and you can add the staff of Mockingjay.net into that mix. I mean, what is the press release going to say? 'People are just dying to try our Cornucopia Coaster!' Are vomit drinks going to be available so you can enjoy your cotton candy and fried Twinkies over and over again?

Meanwhile, others commented that their curiosity was piqued, and that depending on developments they may be compelled by the idea. Some have expressed interest in a focus on the Districts, others suggested Hunger Games-style food like lamb stew could be sold. Needless to say, fans of the series will be waiting for Lionsgate's next call with bated breath.

And what says Suzanne Collins of Lionsgate's packed marketing schedule? Is her message besmirched, lost and trampled? After a long silence, the author finally spoke in an interview with *Variety* on 29 October 2013.

'I'm thrilled with the work Tim Palen and his marketing team have done on the film,' Collins told *Variety* via email. 'It's appropriately disturbing and thought-provoking how the campaign promotes "Catching Fire" while simultaneously promoting the Capitol's punitive forms of entertainment. The stunning image of Katniss in her wedding dress that we use to sell tickets is just the kind of thing the Capitol would use to rev up its audience for the Quarter Quell (the name of the games in "Catching Fire"). That dualistic approach is very much in keeping with the books.'

Dualism and beyond, perhaps *Slate*'s Katie Roiphe said it best:

given the glorious confluence of marketing and message, the fusion of satire and Facebook, one almost wonders if our entire world wasn't written by Suzanne Collins, if there is some great, cosmic library somewhere, where her name is printed discreetly on its spine.

Whether or not we are the Capitol, the fandom continues to fight back against overwhelming marketing methods and Lionsgate's focus on the glitz and glamour of the

Capitol. However, as we move away from *Capitol Couture* towards District 13, Lionsgate is probably preparing for a massive change in tone. I for one will be withholding judgement on these Capitol exploits and awaiting the studio's next move in marketing Panem's upcoming on-screen revolution in *Mockingjay*. ●

~~~~~~~~~~

## GO FURTHER

**Online**

*Hunger Games Fireside Chat*: http://www.hgfiresidechat.com

'"Hunger Games" Theme Park Possible, Says Lionsgate CEO'
Etan Vlessing
*Hollywood Reporter*. 8 November 2013,
http://www.hollywoodreporter.com/news/hunger-games-theme-park-says-654613.

'5 Reasons a "Hunger Games" Theme Park Would Rock Our World'
Jacqueline Burt
*The Stir*. 8 November 2013,
http://thestir.cafemom.com/entertainment/163874/5_reasons_a_hunger_games.

Lionsgate in talks for possible 'The Hunger Games' theme park
Sara Gundell
*The Hunger Games Examiner*. 8 November 2013,
http://www.examiner.com/article/lionsgate-talks-for-possible-the-hunger-games-theme-park

'Please, Let's Not Have a "Hunger Games" Theme Park'
Esther Zuckerman
*Atlantic Wire*. 8 November 2013,
http://www.theatlanticwire.com/entertainment/2013/11/please-lets-not-have-hunger-games-theme-park/71408/.

'Lionsgate Approached For 'Hunger Games' Theme Parks'
Crystal Watanabe
*Mockingjay.net*. 7 November 2013,
http://mockingjay.net/2013/11/08/lionsgate-approached-hunger-games-theme-parks/.

Propos: The Publicity vs The Message

'Suzanne Collins Breaks Silence to Support "The Hunger Games: Catching Fire"'
Marc Graser
*Variety*. 29 October 2013,
http://variety.com/2013/film/news/suzanne-collins-breaks-silence-to-support-the-hunger-games-catching-fire-1200775202/.

'Lionsgate's Tim Palen Crafts Stylish Universe for "Hunger Games: Catching Fire"'
Marc Graser
*Variety*. 29 October 2013,
http://variety.com/2013/biz/news/lionsgates-tim-palen-crafts-stylish-universe-for-hunger-games-catching-fire-1200772931/.

'CoverGirl Helps You Get The Hunger Games Look By Draping You In Weird Feathers, Bits of Twine'
Robert Kessler
*Celebuzz*. 21 October 2013,
http://www.celebuzz.com/2013-10-21/covergirl-helps-you-get-the-hunger-games-look-by-draping-you-in-weird-feathers-bits-of-twine/.

'Is the Capitol Couture Clothing Line Sending the Wrong Message to Hunger Games Fans?'
Emily Asher-Perrin
*Tor.com*. 18 September 2013,
http://www.tor.com/blogs/2013/09/is-the-capitol-couture-clothing-line-sending-the-wrong-message-to-hunger-games-fans.

'Crossing the (Fashion) Line'
The Girl With The Pearl
*Victor's Village*. 5 September 2013,
http://victorsvillage.com/2013/09/05/crossing-the-fashion-line/.

'"Hunger Games: Catching Fire" Victory Tour Posters Revealed'
Angie Han
*/Film*. 22 February 2013,
http://www.slashfilm.com/hunger-games-catching-fire-victory-tour-posters-revealed/.

'The Hunger Games' ignites the ALA's list of most challenged books'
Stephen Lee
*Entertainment Weekly*. 9 April 2012,
http://shelf-life.ew.com/2012/04/09/the-hunger-games-ala-challenged-books/.

'"The Hunger Games": A Glimpse at the Future?'
*Vigilant Citizen*. 5 April 2012,
http://vigilantcitizen.com/moviesandtv/the-hunger-games-a-glimpse-at-the-new-world-order/.

'The Hunger Games contradiction'
Janet Potter
*Christian Century*. 30 March 2012,
http://www.christiancentury.org/blogs/archive/2012-03/hunger-games-contradiction.

'Is *The Hunger Games* Publicity too HungerGames-ish?'
Katie Roiphe
*Slate*. 22 March 2012,
http://www.slate.com/articles/arts/roiphe/2012/03/is_the_publicity_for_the_hunger_games_movie_echoing_the_hunger_games_.html.

'Capitol Control: The Irony of the Hunger Games Movie Mania'
Kelsey Wallace
*Bitch Magazine*. 22 March 2012,
http://bitchmagazine.org/post/capitol-control-the-irony-of-the-hunger-games-movie.

'"Hunger Games" ads coyly don't show the Hunger Games'
Ben Fritz
*Los Angeles Times*. 15 March 2012,
http://articles.latimes.com/2012/mar/15/business/la-fi-ct-hunger-games-marketing-20120316.

'The Hunger Games cut by the BBFC: 13-year-olds should be allowed to see 'splashes of blood''
Brendan O'Neill
*The Telegraph*. 13 March 2012,
http://blogs.telegraph.co.uk/news/brendanoneill2/100143504/the-hunger-games-cut-by-the-bbfc-13-year-olds-should-be-allowed-to-see-splashes-of-blood/.

'The Hunger Games' (Official release information from BBFC): http://www.bbfc.co.uk/releases/hunger-games-5

'Catching Fire' (Official release information from BBFC): http://www.bbfc.co.uk/releases/hunger-games-catching-fire-film

# Fan Appreciation no.2
# Adam Spunberg & Savanna New of the
## *Hunger Games Fireside Chat Podcast*

Adam Spunberg and Savanna New are friends and New Yorkers with a passion for *The Hunger Games*. Together they launched the *Hunger Games Fireside Chat* podcast in April 2011, a weekly discussion about everything from casting news to fans' crackpot theories. The format is inspired by the informal, familiar style of Franklin D. Roosevelt's series of 'fireside chat' radio addresses and airs live on Monday nights at 10 p.m. EST at *hgfiresidechat.com*.

**Nicola Balkind (NB):** Simple things first, how did you first hear about and read The Hunger Games?

**Adam Spunberg (AS):** I was – this may shock you – also a Harry Potter (J.K. Rowling, 1997-2007) fan in addition to The Hunger Games. I moved to New York in 2009 and was basically just trying to get to know more people, socialize, integrate myself into my new community. So I joined a Harry Potter club, actually made a really close friend named Ariel who was a huge Hunger Games fan and kept pushing me to read them. I told Savanna what Ariel said, Savanna read them, and she really liked them and strongly encouraged me too. After a lot of insisting I finally read the first book, and then read the first two very quickly. When the third one came out I read it right away.

**Savanna New (SN):** Yeah I just heard about them through Adam. I was not and still am not really a huge fan of YA [young adult] literature, but I did really love Harry Potter and Adam mentioned that people were touting The Hunger Games as 'the next Harry Potter' so I thought oh, well I'll give these a try. You know how they just suck you in immediately, and I think I read the first two books in maybe a couple of weeks – then I only had to wait a month or so for *Mockingjay* to come out, which was nice, since some people had to wait a year!

**NB:** I know what you mean – I got lucky and started reading right as *Mockingjay* just came out so was able to marathon them. So what was it that you recognized as unique about the series and that really hooked you in or made you want to continue your relationship with it?

**SN:** Well first of all I'd never read anything quite like The Hunger Games before. That was right before the big YA dystopia trend started so I was so struck by how relevant it was to what we're seeing today in our society. Of course that was Suzanne Collins's intent – she was inspired by the Iraq War and reality television – and I thought it was such an inspired theme, and very brave in a way. You know, there aren't a lot of people writing books that address deep topics like that for young adults. So I thought that was really compelling, because that is an issue that exists today. People are very blinded to the realities of the world, they only care about entertainment and things like that. You know, the whole '*panem et circences*, bread and circuses' – as long as people are entertained and fed, who cares about politics and social issues? Obviously the trilogy presents that idea in a very extreme way, but it's completely something that I see today, and I feel like, Adam, you could say the same?

**AS:** Absolutely. I will say that we did sense that this was going to be something tremendous. But the reason we thought that is because it was good; it wasn't just that we rode this popularity wave that we foresaw. So I think what it was for me was that I hadn't read anything that suspenseful in years. I know that's not necessarily a praise to everybody, obviously it has a plethora of other qualities, that wasn't all it had. But I thought in terms of a truly engaging story, where you were absolutely breathless, on the edge of your seat and just barely able to tolerate what would happen next. What was an accomplishment for me, and what I've actually used as inspiration for some of my own writing, was that I truly did not realize when one chapter ended and the next one began – that's how sucked in I was. I think her ability as a storyteller is remarkable, and truly she's ahead of the whole class.

**SN:** I would say the other thing that drew both of us in, I assume this is true for most Hunger Games fans, is the character of Katniss. She's so real – she's very flawed, she is relatable in that way, I think, she's not just the traditional heroine that you see …

**AS:** [deadpan] Not true, actually. I hate her and I like every aspect of the story except for the part where she's in it.

**SN:** Oh God. [laughter] But no, that character was so brilliantly created by Suzanne Collins and despite her flaws she has such a strength and resilience that's admirable and that I think people feel inspired by. Another thing that really drew me in is the way that Collins plays with gender roles. We have Katniss who takes on this more traditionally masculine role, whereas Peeta is the kind of physically weaker person, but who's more skilled with speaking and things like that. I liked that she did that, because you do not see that very often in young adult literature.

**NB:** It's funny you bring that up because I've just been writing about gender today and one blog in particular was very concerned about the so-called 'gender flipping' in the series.

**SN:** I think what's so amazing about it is that it's those qualities that make Peeta so loved by everyone. I would venture to say he's the most loved character in the whole trilogy. Suzanne Collins is a brilliant storyteller across the board.

**AS:** He's a great guy. I mean, what are his flaws? He's such a nice guy but at the same time he also has his own morals, which he clearly sticks to – like in the famous scene where he says 'I just want to be me'. So I think he's terrific and what I like is, speaking as a guy, is that I wasn't the most Gale-like growing up – not the hunter, so to speak – I like that people are looking up to Peeta because he's a great role model and male sensitivity shouldn't be completely shunned the way that some people do.

**NB:** I think that's something which is fairly unspoken in the fandom. A lot is made about Katniss being a strong female character but very few people talk about Peeta as a more vulnerable male character.

**SN:** Katniss gets a lot of flack from a lot of people for being so unemotional and stoic, and that's only in relation to the other standard female protagonists that you get. It's interesting how she defies expectations in a way that makes some people uncomfortable, because I think they aren't used to seeing a girl who isn't crying over everything.

**NB:** I'm guessing you've both reread the series more than once. Did you have any major changes in perspective during your second or third reading?

**AS:** I actually went out of my way to try not to reread it too many times. I know that runs contrary to what a lot of people try to do. I wanted to keep the story not so fresh in my mind so as I could enjoy the movies. [On the podcast] we've gone through so many aspects and pages of the story over and over again. We've even got a promotion called 'Pick a Page' where Savanna 'claims' to randomly pick a page – just kidding, she's very honourable – using a number generator and we analyse it with our panelists.

In retrospect the biggest thing that has changed for me is just that we're looking at it through such a different lens since becoming part of this fandom, and becoming part of this fansite world and in the podcast, that honestly we no longer look at it, I think, purely as a reading fan perspective. There's a more administrative role, almost like we're part of the project. Sometimes we've felt like part of the whole franchise and cogs in the engine – we like to think of ourselves that way anyway – and I think that makes us view it with a sense of ownership, even, sometimes. Maybe it's foolish but we do.

**SN:** What's interesting for me is that honestly nothing has really changed for me. I've reread the series a couple of times now and it's been just as incredible each time. Which is interesting because usually when I reread something I feel that I like it more or not as much. But for The Hunger Games I don't know – my experience hasn't really changed. I think we've picked up on some more details here and there.

**NB:** Have you had any experience with in-person Hunger Games meet-ups?

**SN:** Last year Lionsgate invited us to attend the world premiere of *The Hunger Games* in Los Angeles. Adam and I went out there and we rented a house for the weekend with some people from the fansite *Down With the Capitol* and there were twelve fansites total, I believe, who had been invited. So we spent the whole weekend hanging out and had a big party with people from every single fansite, basically, so in that sense it was a meet-up. It was weird we were being followed by a camera crew so we filmed some stuff and we did a live stream there for *Fireside Chat*. Also that weekend before the premiere, Lionsgate allowed a certain number of fans to camp out in order to get tickets and they gave us Lionsgate staff-access to hang out at the camp, talk to the fans, meet some of the cast and everything. I haven't been to any conventions or anything but obviously we had a lot of Hunger Games related discussion and everything there.

**NB:** There don't seem to be any dedicated Hunger Games meet-ups except surrounding their events or, say, the panel at San Diego Comic Con (2013).

**SN:** There are definitely Harry Potter-centric conventions right now but there is no Hunger Games only convention right now. Fans have tried to start one and allegedly they were shut down by Lionsgate so I don't know if that's ever going to happen, but maybe someday!

**NB:** Who are some of your favourite guests you've had on the podcast?

**SN:** We've had so many that it's easy to lose track. One of my favourite guests, and this was fresh in my mind, we had the author of a wilderness survival guide themed around The Hunger Games. This guy was so cool, his name is Creek Stewart and the book is *The Unofficial Hunger Games Wilderness Survival Guide* (2013). He came on and I just loved him because when we interview people about projects, books, whatever, we talk about the project – but he, in addition to that, was actually able to teach us some very valuable survival lessons. I feel like I learned so much from him even though he was only on for like 10 or 15 minutes. He was really cool. Let's see, who else? In terms of cast members, we have done interviews but it has not been audio for the show, it's been written.

**AS:** I really enjoyed Ned Vizzini, we even prepared a funny script with him beforehand. Remember how much fun that was?

**SN:** Yeah. He's an author, he wrote *It's Kind of a Funny Story* (2006), and we had him on because he'd contributed to *The Girl Who Was On Fire* (ed Leah Wilson, 2011). So he came on to talk about his essay, which was about reality TV, and he was just really fun to talk to. He was a great guest.

**AS:** He was terrific. We've had a lot of really interesting people within the fandom that we relished having as guests. There's a group of people who do an audio production called *The Katniss Chronicles*, and they're just delightful people. We actually hung out with them on our trip to LA. Well, one guest – if you want to call it that – is now defunct but now is kind of a big deal, and that's Gamemaker of a game called …

**NB:** From *Panem October*! Yeah, we'll have a chapter on that, it's a fascinating story.

**AS:** His thing was so big, what he had going at its absolute height. We helped him out a bit with the project and he had some extraordinary plans. It's sad that it never came to fruition because it would have been really amazing.

**Fan Appreciation no.2**
Adam Spunberg & Savanna New

**NB:** It seemed pretty beloved. What are some of the most meaningful responses you've had from fans, either to the podcast or in discussion?

**SN:** There have been a lot. The thing is it has been two years so we get emails from people thanking us for the show and telling us how it makes their week. We got an e-mail not long ago from a mother whose son is autistic and he has difficulty relating to people and talking to people, but The Hunger Games is something he's really passionate about, and listening to our show every week gives him a chance to connect with people who are as passionate about the series. She was thanking us for that, which was really sweet. People really feel very strongly about this series. It touches people in a profound way, I think.

**AS:** To follow up on that, the e-mail from the parent was really touching. Honestly, I think some of the fervour has died down a bit since there was such a gap between the first and second film. Lately we've done the show a lot more from the perspective of just having fun with this and not worrying so much about who's listening and the reactions – although we do still get plenty of good feedback. But when the show was at its absolute height, probably during the build-up to the first movie and for a couple of months after that, we used to get comments all the time and a really active chat list, people tweeting all the time. It was one of the most rewarding things I'd say I experienced in my life. It's funny, you wonder why people would be interested in what you have to say about anything, and people say really nice things.

At the same time what Savanna and I always try to do is to put across that we're really still just fans for the fun of it, we just have this platform. As Savanna has alluded to, we're friends with all the other fansites, and that has probably been the thing that has been most exciting about this. Obviously the ebbs and flows of life will change some of that but I think there's a good chance that at least a few of us are going to be lifelong friends, which is really special.

**NB:** This relates to an answer you gave in a *Down With The Capitol* interview a long time ago. You said that you hope as the fandom grows that we remember that it's still community-based and everyone is so nice. Do you feel that's still true?

**AS:** I think so, mostly. There have been a few defectors, as you might expect [laughter] but the core people that Savanna and I talk to are all still friends. It's something that's really special. For example, a couple of people are coming to New York for us to see the movie together on opening night, just to have that sense of community, and I wouldn't have known them if not for the podcast.

The biggest regret that Savanna and I have is not being able to go to LA for the premiere this year. We were invited but financially it was too much of a burden for each of us (and I should tell you that we don't make money on this at all, by the way). We really just regretted not getting to see each other.

My favourite episode we ever did wasn't over the phone, it was the live Ustream that we did from Los Angeles the night before the premiere. Everyone was on it and it was a chance for everyone to be there together, partaking in this incredible excitement. It's really sad to me that we're not getting to do it this time around, but I'm still hopeful that maybe with *Mockingjay* or especially *Mockingjay: Part 2* so that we can have a last hurrah where all of us will be together. I think that would really prove how solid our tightknit friendships really are. I'll just add that we talk about things way beyond The Hunger Games. These are friends we can confide very personal things to.

**SN:** Absolutely, yeah, they're real friends.

**NB:** What do you think it is about The Hunger Games that brings people together?

**SN:** I think it's like anything that has a fan base around it. Every fan of The Hunger Games love this series very passionately and when you love something that much you can't help but want to connect with other people who feel the same way. The Hunger Games especially, there's so much to discuss and I think that it lends itself to people coming together and talking about it. I think it's something that brings up a lot of dialogue that people enjoy getting into. The trilogy itself is about people coming together, so I think that's reflected in the fandom. It's about uniting for a common cause, and that's what we see in the fan base.

**AS:** I think there's a deeper mission behind Suzanne Collins's books than maybe some of the other series. I'm not trying to put down Harry Potter, I love Harry Potter, as do many people in the fandom, but I think there are some strong moral lessons that can be taken from not only Collins's words, but the movies even push that further by showing you a lot of the perspective of the Capitol. I think it relates a lot about our issues that can strike people in the same way.

It's interesting how, for instance, one of the major American themes pre-9/11 was this suburban angst sort of thing and people were able to relate to different things. I think now there's a lot of concern about global problems, oppressive governments in the sense of the Internet, reality television – which of course The Hunger Games has a massive corollary to in the story. So I think it points out a lot of the vices that if we don't change certain things about how our current society is going it's not so far-fetched that Panem could exist someday in the future. Yet you want a cause for hope. There are so many people who are going to The Hunger Games and believing in the positive mission that maybe we have a chance against horrors of global warming and whatever else might come our way.

## GO FURTHER

### Books

*The Girl Who Was on Fire*
ed Leah Wilson
(Dallas: Smart Pop Books , 2011)

*The Unofficial Hunger Games Wilderness Survival Guide*
Creek Stewart
(Blue Ash, OH: Betterway Books, 2013)

*It's Kind of a Funny Story*
Ned Vizzini
(New York, New York: Hyperion, 2006)

### Online

Websites
*Hunger Games Fireside Chat*, http://www.hgfiresidechat.com
*The Fandom*, http://thefandom.net/
*The Katniss Chronicles*, http://www.thekatnisschronicles.com/
*Down With The Capitol*, http://hungergamesdwtc.net/
*Mainstay Pro*, http://www.youtube.com/user/MainstayPro/videos
*The Potter Games*, http://thepottergames.com/

# SO IT'S YOU AND A SYRINGE AGAINST THE CAPITOL? SEE, THIS IS WHY NO ONE LETS YOU MAKE THE PLANS.

**HAYMITCH ABERNATHY**
CATCHING FIRE

# Chapter
## 5

# Race & Representation
# in Panem & Beyond

→ Issues of race and representation, in Panem and in the real world, are perhaps the most controversial topics to hit the Hunger Games fandom. A great debate was sparked during the casting of The Hunger Games movie, and was redoubled in the wake of the film's release. Let's explore the backlash and key discussions about race that took place in the public arena and Hunger Games fandom.

(You can find a fantastic, in-depth literary examination of race and its place in Panem as part of The Hunger Games canon in Chapter 3 of 2012's *The Panem Companion* by V. Arrow.)

Suzanne Collins's descriptions of characters, particularly those in District 12, are present but vague. Katniss describes herself as having the typical Seam look: olive skin, straight black hair and grey eyes. This intentionally vague description has been the source of debate for fans, with myriad groups claiming ownership of the Seam and its residents. Katniss is considered by some readers to be of Native American, Mediterranean, Asian, Latin, or mixed descent. Many were angry, then, when Jennifer Lawrence – a blonde Caucasian woman – was cast in the role of Katniss. In fact, the role of Katniss was deliberately cast as white. A *Wall Street Journal* article quotes the casting call thus:

[casting agent] Ms. Zane's staff has posted the single paragraph laying out the filmmakers' broad criteria for Katniss. She should be Caucasian, between ages 15 and 20, who could portray someone 'underfed but strong,' and 'naturally pretty underneath her tomboyishness.'

The casting director's choice to dismiss non-Caucasian actors for the role of Katniss is a troubling indicator of a larger racial bias in Hollywood. The act has been depicted as 'whitewashing' across mainstream media websites, fansites and personal blogs. There has been a great deal of online discussion surrounding recent 'race bending' casting decisions, including *The Last Airbender* (Shyamalan, 2010) and *Drive* (Winding Refn, 2011) which both saw white actors cast in the roles of characters of colour (see 'Hollywood Whitewashing (Yes, It Really Hurts)' in *Geek Quality*). As we touched upon in Chapter 3 on Katniss and gender issues, movies with a female lead are seen as a risk in Hollywood. Presumably, from a movie studio's point of view, this issue would be compounded by the further decision to cast a woman of colour in a leading role.

After initial upset stirred, Suzanne Collins said little to quell the flames of the debate. As she told *Entertainment Weekly*:

They [Katniss and Gale] were not particularly intended to be biracial. It is a time period where hundreds of years have passed from now. There's been a lot of ethnic mixing. But I think I describe them as having dark hair, grey eyes, and sort of olive skin. You know, we have hair and makeup. But then there are some characters in the book who are more specifically described.

She goes on to say that Thresh and Rue, for example, are African-American. Rue is introduced by Katniss thus: 'She has dark brown skin and eyes, but other than that, she's very like Prim in size and demeanour.' It is this description that caused the biggest furore in the fandom to date.

Race & Representation in Panem & Beyond

Some fans who had watched the movie expressed their surprise and dismay that some characters were portrayed by black actors. Two major articles by *Jezebel* and *Inquisitr* were written in response, and these authors did not hesitate to label some negative reactors as racist. A spate of articles shared screenshots of some of the most egregious comments on Twitter. A guest poster on *Racialicious* also weighed in, giving a less sensational sample of tweets and views but expressing the disappointment in their fellow fans. Many of those commenting on Twitter complained that Rue had not been described as dark-skinned in the book (though, in fact, she was). A Tumblr blog called *Hunger Games Tweets* was also set up, which blogged tweets and comments about these issues of race. The blogger who runs this Tumblr account also wrote that they were scared and dismayed by the reactions, saying that (original emphasis):

*Fig. 1: Fan Art which reinterperets Katniss and Rue as women of colour.*

> All these … people … read the Hunger Games. Clearly, they all fell in love with and cared about Rue. Though what they really fell in love with was an image of Rue that they'd created in their minds. A girl that they knew they could love and adore and mourn at the thought of knowing that she's been brutally killed … These people are MAD that the girl that they cried over while reading the book was 'some black girl' all along. So now they're angry. Wasted tears, wasted emotions. It's sad to think that had they known that she was black all along, there would have been [no] sorrow or sadness over her death. There are MAJOR TIE-INS to these reactions and the injustices that we see around the world today.

This is a stark example which demonstrates that fans relate to the likes of Katniss and Rue because they are unconventional heroes, set apart from other heroines in the genre because they are described as people of colour.

Despite the fevered debate surrounding the casting of Rue, little was said about Lenny Kravitz's turn as Katniss's stylist Cinna. However one anonymous fan on *Yahoo! Answers* posited the following:

> So, as you hopefully know, Lenny Kravitz is the actor who has been chosen to play Cinna in the Hunger Games. But the thing is, he's totally not what I imagined Cinna as. To be quite frank… I imagined Cinna being white. And nowhere throughout the entire series did it even mention he had dark skin… So did you imagine Cinna as being white? Black? Any other race in particular? I just thought that it wasn't good a good [*sic*] choice choosing an actor that didn't fit the book's description.

In fact, Cinna is described as having short brown hair and green eyes with gold flecks. Katniss is 'taken aback by how normal he looks' compared with his fellow high-fashion

73

Fig. 2: One fan recast characters from District 12 on Tumblr.

Fig. 3: A popular meme expresses distaste for the casting of The Hunger Games.

Capitol dwellers, but she does not mention his skin colour. This response is interesting because it posits that Collins's characters should be white by default, and only darker-skinned if specifically noted. Others have assumed that 'Cinna' is a play on or shortening of 'cinnamon'. On the whole, where Cinna is mentioned in articles about race, he is skimmed over to get to the meatier Rue argument. As Denise Warner of *Hollywood Life* puts it, 'Cinna's race is never strictly defined, but how can anyone doubt Lenny Kravitz's appeal.'

Far from dwelling on their dismay at the racist few, however, fans have found their own ways to experience *The Hunger Games* as they imagined it while reading. Some took the issue of poor casting into their own hands and have reimagined the Panem universe with likenesses, particularly of famous actors, who they would cast as the characters from the book series. Many of these are based on Suzanne Collins's descriptions of the characters, and are recast in relation to the individual's reading of these descriptions. For example, a Tumblr user named Leah (Tumblr user ghostofharrenhal) recast characters from District 12 in a post called 'The Seam: Recast'. Her ideal line-up recasts American actress and signer Q'orianka Kilcher, whose roles have included Pocahontas in Terrence Malick's *The New World* (2005) and the title character of *Princess Kaiulani* (Marc Forby, 2009), the nineteenth-century Crown Princess of Hawaii. Meanwhile she recasts Haymitch, played by Woody Harrelson in the films, as Native American actor Zahn McClarnon. In the tags, Leah writes, '#i just wanted my screen to be filled with native people and instead it was filled with white people.' Her profile references her being of Native American descent, specifically Piegan Blackfeet. This kind of fan activity demonstrates the deep level of personal identification that fans have found in The Hunger Games series. While many of Suzanne Collins's characters are described by the author as 'olive-skinned', 'grey eyed', and so on, the predominantly white casting of the movie left many fans feeling betrayed.

Feelings of upset are demonstrated in a suite of blog posts and social media posts, including key memes like Katniss in the centre of a colour wheel which reads, 'Movie about institutionalized oppression – change the main character to white.' Unlike some of the irate messages sent by surprised fans after watching the film, these commentaries on race are, for the most part, intelligently and delicately argued. Fans participating in these kinds of discussions have expressed great interest in the reception, and possible perceptions, of the film's representations of race. Some have argued that seeing people of colour interact on-screen would bring greater depth to the story by shirking the mainstream. It's an important argument: what if the same scene was played out with characters played by people of colour? What new levels of nuance can be brought to readings of the story? While many readers clearly imagined key characters as white despite their descriptions, there are hundreds of ways to read key scenes while putting racial diversity into play. One fan named Emma (iconsidermyself on Tumblr) blogged on the subject, arguing that there is potential for greater nuance here. In a blog post using

Race & Representation in Panem & Beyond

the above-mentioned Katniss meme as a header, Emma writes:

> Jennifer Lawrence is a great actress and she did a wonderful job in the role of Katniss. That being said, I would have preferred a biracial actress to play this part because I can think of so few heroines with 'olive colored skin' that when one finally appears she ought not to be white washed.
> Think how much more incredible the scene where Katniss covers Rue in flowers would have been if Katniss and Rue were both women of color. Think how much more powerful it would be if it weren't a white woman mourning the loss of a black woman. (We've seen that before. We've seen privileged characters learn from less privileged ones.) Think how amazing it would be for women of color to see themselves represented in every scene that Rue and Katniss share. The Hunger Games has already shown itself to be an incredibly popular film. Just imagine if such a successful film contained scenes which included only actresses of color. I would trade in Jennifer Lawrence's performance for that.

Another Tumblr user by the name of silkchemise has written extensively on the subject of race and representation in *The Hunger Games*, and uses the same topic as a jumping-off point to discuss the portrayal of people of colour in all types of media and art. She also commentates on the use of stereotypes and typical portrayals of people of colour in the media, and the ways that race relations operate within the storyworld of Panem. In online discussions, the writer often invites readers to imagine the familiar story with people of different races in each of the roles, adding new dimensions to her argument through the continual recasting of characters by race throughout the text. For example:

> Johanna Mason is one of my favorite characters in the series; as a woman of Color myself, it would be great to see someone who looked like me playing her. (Then again, Katniss is one of my favorites as well; shouldn't she have looked like me, too?) But put the wise-cracking, sarcastic, scantily-clad, brown Johanna against Jennifer Lawrence, and now she just feels like a 'sassy Black woman' stereotype or a tired 'spicy Latina' trope.

Putting it all into perspective, she continues:

> The racist casting of 'The Hunger Games' has put the casting of 'Catching Fire' in a catch-22. This franchise does not need more White people, thank you. The previous film did a bang-up job of that. But now that Our Heroes are White, any role given to a PoC will be destroyed by the film's new racial power structure (one hugely different from that of the books) [...] the terrible casting choices of the first film made everything a whooooole lot more complicated. And frankly, I don't even know what

the solution is.

While this fan puzzles over a solution, many more fans have expressed themselves for or in opposition to the racial constructions of The Hunger Games movie casting, and some have done so through cosplay.

Effie Trinket is a popular cosplay character. Katniss, upon seeing Effie Trinket, narrates, 'Effie Trinket, District 12's escort, fresh from the Capitol with her scary white grin, pinkish hair and spring green suit.' In the films she is played by Elizabeth Banks, dressed and made up in the Capitol fashion with colourful flourishes and her face powdered snow white. Meanwhile a fan by the name of Mahogany H., or Mitsu-Neko on DeviantArt, plays with the character of Effie Trinket in a way that places her in striking contrast to the movie casting. She plays a dark-skinned Effie in her trade-marked bright wigs and colourful eyeshadows. At the time of writing, on Mahogany's DeviantArt profile, she expresses her excitement for the impending *Catching Fire* movie release and states that she has made another Effie outfit, her fifth. She has also cosplayed with her boyfriend as Haymitch. Under one image in her album from Anime North 2012 she writes, 'I really loved cosplaying Effie, it was so easy to be in character, and I've never been stopped so often for pics!' Her image appeared on one niche cosplay Tumblr dedicated to black cosplayers called cosplayingwhileblack. Similar communities include the following Tumblr handles: cross-race-cosplay, cosplayindominicanrepublic, and cosplayingwhilelatino.

While Mahogany's cosplay seems to be free of political motivations (she has not referenced or accompanied any of her images with mentions of race), one Canadian cosplayer named Pan had a very personally emotional response to news that Katniss was described as olive-skinned, and it spurred her into action. As she writes in her profile, 'I am also engaged in social justice-related issues and do a lot of work that involves making sense of and combating structural oppression.' Pan's Katniss costume recreates Katniss's Girl on Fire moment during the chariot ride where the Tributes are introduced to the Capitol. In her blog post featuring the costume, she writes passionately about her portrayal of Katniss. She was surprised to find some fanart which portrayed Katniss with dark skin and went on to learn about the issues around the film's casting. Pan soon felt compelled to inhabit the character. In her own words (original emphasis):

Do you know the last time I ran into a female protagonist described as having olive skin and dark hair? Never. I know this because I've been searching for such a protagonist my entire life. I really don't know how to describe it, but when characters in popular culture don't ever look anything like you, it can do something to your head. It can make you feel like you never belong. It can make you long for characters that look like you. It can make your heart ache.
So finding Katniss meant a lot to me. I cried in relief and joy because *it meant that much.*

Race & Representation in Panem & Beyond

Fig. 4 & 5: Fan memes point out that Peeta's injury is not mentioned in the film adaptations.

To be honest, when I read the books, I didn't imagine Katniss looking that much like me, but she *could* look like me, and that's huge.

And I knew I wanted to cosplay her. Cosplaying can be a way to show how much a character means to you, and as a cosplayer, cosplaying Katniss is a way I can show my appreciation for the character. Also, I wanted to cosplay her because of what she represents in the books: a spark, fire, hope, determination.

As the blogger behind the *Hunger Games Tweets* Tumblr account points out, both the fans who expressed surprise and disappointment about Rue's casting and those who had similar views of the white-washing of Katniss had all read, loved and identified with The Hunger Games book series and awaited the movie with the same excitement and anticipation. These reactions from across the spectrum demonstrate the breadth of race issues which The Hunger Games brings up. Non-specific descriptions mean that Katniss could be Native American, biracial, Melungeon, or any combination thereof. More importantly, Katniss's identification as Seam, in opposition to Merchant class, takes place within the book and, due to casting choices, will not play out in what some fans feel is a sufficient or satisfying way on-screen.

But it is not only representations of race which have riled fans and spurred readers into active discussions online. Disability is also an issue which has been diluted in the adaptation from book to film. Katniss meets a few disabled characters including a one-armed woman named Ripper, a trader in the Hob who was injured in a mining accident. While this character has not appeared in *The Hunger Games* film, deeper issues of disability have been glossed over, often to the detriment of storytelling. One fan and professional commentator named s.e. smith wrote an article on the website *Tiger Beatdown* entitled 'So, How ABOUT Those Hunger Games' exploring the disability-focused narrative within *The Hunger Games*. Smith points out that Panem is a physically demanding world in which injury and disability occur in speciality work and the Hunger Games Arena and that 'this is discussed frankly, though not always well, in the books. I wasn't always delighted with the way Collins handled disability, but at least she confronted it'. In the book, Peeta loses a leg due to injuries sustained in the Arena and must undertake the Victory Tour in a prosthesis. In the movie, his injuries are far less severe. Smith writes:

But the decision to alter the storyline with Peeta's leg really troubles me because of what it symbolises. Peeta becomes a prominently disabled character in the series, and his disability becomes part of his experiences. At the same time though, he's not defined by the disability, consumed by it, and placed in the narrative for the sole purpose of constantly reminding everyone that he's disabled. Peeta, like other characters, is scarred by the world he lives in, and he bears a visible mark of the cruelty and brutality of Panem, but more importantly, he's another person trying to survive and build a better world. By neatly cutting that entire plotline away, the filmmakers avoided some tangled and thorny issues.

The writer goes on to look at the issue of Peeta as a love interest, and some prospective issues such as film-makers feeling that his grappling with the injury would take up precious screen time. In the books, Peeta's ongoing depression is related to Katniss, not his injury. In fact, both characters struggle with disabilities in the books which have been magically fixed in the movie. But how does this affect fans' identification with the text? Tumblr user thelegalizeddeafies reblogged a positive reaction to Smith's piece, adding further commentary on the topic of Katniss's deafness also being washed over in the film. The blogger, who is also deaf, expresses a happy identification with the portrayal of Katniss moving on with her new difficulty with hearing, stating that it was an important part of her character and 'another great aspect of how disability was handled' in the books. The reaction reads (original emphasis):

> as a deaf individual i loved this, because so often hearing people think AND say that losing their hearing would be the end of the world, no life could go on. but here in the midst of this atrocious situation, this girl loses a significant portion of her hearing 'permanently' and she doesnt [sic] sit there and cry about it, she CONTINUES TO SURVIVE and do so in extremely hospitable circumstances.

The writer also goes on to point out that, when the Capitol fixes Katniss's loss of hearing after the Hunger Games and before she is conscious, this creates an important parallel with deaf issues in the real world.

> The fact that the Capitol FIXES her hearing WITHOUT her consent, is to any deaf individual a very important and RELEVANT message about the pathological view of deafness that it MUST be fixed, and its not your choice to do so, it is OURS, and the so called 'cure' for deafness and forcing it on people and especially children WITHOUT their consent.

While the disability debate hasn't raged as loudly as that of race, it has become an important part of the wider discourse surrounding *The Hunger Games*, particularly in these key, stark differences in translation from book to film. In fact, so far the only disabled character to be shown on-screen is Quarter Quell Tribute Chaff in *Catching Fire*, who lost a hand in the 45th Hunger Games and refused a prosthetic – but blink and you'll miss it. Meanwhile other fans have engaged in play surrounding the topic of disability, with a Paralympics-style role playing game which took place on *The Hunger Games Wiki*, showing that not only disabled readers have engaged with this topic and taken it on as a facet of their online role play.

We will take a closer look at online and physical role play in Chapter 9 on fan creation.

Race & Representation in Panem & Beyond

Similar issues of the discordance between readings of the book and the casting and, more specifically, marketing of the movies are tackled in Chapter 4. In the meantime, fans will have to wait and see how Lionsgate proceeds with its racial dynamics and treatment of disabilities in the upcoming films – and I trust that the fandom will continue to have its say on these matters in the same compelling manner. ●

~~~~~~~~~~~~~

## GO FURTHER

### Books

The Panem Companion: From Mellark Bakery to Mockingjays
V. Arrow
(Dallas: Smart Pop Books, 2012)

### Online

'Welcome To The 1st Annual Disabled Games'
66mc
*The Hunger Games Wiki.* 27 October 2012,
http://thehungergames.wikia.com/wiki/User_blog:66mc/The_1st_Disabled_Games.

'Hunger Games Actor Is Ignoring the Racist Haters'
Dodai Stewart
*Jezebel.* 2 April 2012,
http://jezebel.com/5898419/hunger-games-actor-is-ignoring-the-racist-haters.

'Racist "Hunger Games" Fans Clearly Can't Read'
Denise Warner
*Hollywood Life.* 29 March 2012, http://hollywoodlife.com/2012/03/29/hunger-games-racist-tweets-amandla-stenberg/.

'Bad News: Hunger Games' Amandla Stenberg Knows About the Racist Tweets'
Dodai Stewart
*Jezebel.* 29 March 2012,
http://jezebel.com/5897416/bad-news-hunger-games-amandla-stenberg-knows-about-the-racist-tweets.

'That Awkward Moment When Racism In The Hunger Games Fandom Reflects A Deeper

Sickness'
Page Mackinley
*Inquisitr*. 28 March 2012,
http://www.inquisitr.com/212536/hunger-games-fandom-racism/.

'I loved this essay about disability & The Hunger Games'
*The Legalized Deafies* [Tumblr]
27 March 2012, http://thelegalizeddeafies.tumblr.com/post/20043717334/i-loved-this-essay-about-disability-the-hunger-games.

'Recap: The Everdeen in the room'
Tanya
*Geek Quality*. 26 March 2012,
http://www.geekquality.com/recap/.

'Racist *Hunger Games* Fans Are Very Disappointed'
Dodai Stewart
*Jezebel*. 26 March 2012,
http://jezebel.com/5896408/racist-hunger-games-fans-dont-care-how-much-money-the-movie-made.

'A Character-By-Character Guide to Race in *The Hunger Games*'
Dodai Stewart
*Jezebel*. 26 March 2012,
http://jezebel.com/5896515/a-character+by+character-guide-to-race-in-the-hunger-games.

'In the Hunger Games, what happens to disabled competitors?'
*Quora*. 26 March 2012,
http://www.quora.com/The-Hunger-Games-2008-book/In-the-Hunger-Games-what-happens-to-disabled-competitors.

'So How ABOUT Those Hunger Games?'
s.e. smith
*Tiger Beatdown*. 26 March 2012,
http://www.tigerbeatdown.com/2012/03/26/so-how-about-those-hunger-games.

'Gender & Food Week: "The Hunger Games" Review in Conversation: Female Protagonists, Body Image, Disability, Whitewashing, Hunger & Food'
*Bitch Flicks*. 24 December 2012,

Race & Representation in Panem & Beyond

http://www.btchflcks.com/2012/12/gender-and-food-week-the-hunger-games-review-in-conversation.html.

'Hollywood Whitewashing (Yes, It Really Hurts)'
Elyse
Geek Quality. 22 March 2012,
http://www.geekquality.com/hollywood-whitewashing/.

'All racial inequality aside... did you imagine Cinna from the Hunger Games as being black?'
Yahoo! Answers [n.d.], http://answers.yahoo.com/question/index?qid=20111104193338A
Aci8ef.

'Team "Hunger Games" talks: Author Suzanne Collins and director Gary Ross on their allegiance to each other, and their actors – EXCLUSIVE'
Karen Valby
Entertainment Weekly. 7 April 2011,
http://insidemovies.ew.com/2011/04/07/hunger-games-suzanne-collins-gary-ross-exclusive/.

'Yes, There Are Black People in Your Hunger Games: The Strange Case of Rue & Cinna'
Racialicious. 15 November 2011,
http://www.racialicious.com/2011/11/15/yes-there-are-black-people-in-your-hunger-games-the-strange-case-of-rue-cinna/

'The Newcomers'
John Jurgensen
Wall Street Journal. 25 February 2011,
http://online.wsj.com/news/articles/SB10001424052748703529004576160782323146
532.

'The Seam: Recast', ghostofharrenhal [Tumblr]. [n.d.],
http://ghostofharrenhal.tumblr.com/post/20470212855/the-seam-recast-primrose-everdeen-played-by.

[Untitled], iconsidermyself [Tumblr]. 25 March 2012,
http://iconsidermyself.tumblr.com/post/19921001132/jennifer-lawrence-is-a-great-actress-and-she-did-a

'Katniss Opression Meme', silkchemise [Tumblr]. [n.d.]

http://silkchemise.tumblr.com/post/20316914291/alemonlemoned-michelleeeeen.

'Gary Ross Ruined everything', *silkchemise* [Tumblr]. [n.d.]
http://silkchemise.tumblr.com/tagged/tldr%3A-gary-ross-ruined-everything.

'Silkchemise on Katniss identifying as Seam', *silkchemise* [Tumblr]. [n.d.],
http://silkchemise.tumblr.com/post/24956677191/katniss-may-not-be-able-to-be-classified-as.

'Silkchemise on President Snow', *silkchemise* [Tumblr], [n.d.], http://silkchemise.tumblr.com/post/25259693495/the-colors-are-lovely-of-course-but-nothing-says.

*Cosplay*
Pan as Katniss Everdeen: http://www.lelola.net/cosplay/katnissparade/index.html; http://www.lelola.net/cosplay/about.html ; http://katnissisoliveskinneddealwithit.tumblr.com/post/37440506882/weve-posted-some-of-elementalkatniss-cosplaying

Mahogany H. as Effie Trinket: http://mitsu-neko.deviantart.com/

Chapter
6

# Fan Philosophies & Activism: *The Hunger Games* for Social Good

→ Two key themes in Suzanne Collins's The Hunger Games series are inequality and poverty. The first instalment was released in 2008 during a recession landscape and around the time of the 2008 economic crash, and the series has been building cultural resonance in the years that follow. These real world issues have grown in stark relation to those within the novels, and even more so in the run-up to and during the release of The Hunger Games film in 2012.

In The Hunger Games and Catching Fire, Romanesque Capitol citizens wear ridiculous finery, host grand parties and feasts, and even use a vomitorium-inspired drink to allow them to purge and then gorge themselves anew over the course of an evening. Meanwhile poor, would-be Tribute children in the Districts face starvation, including our heroine Katniss, who is one example of a child going rogue to feed her family. One share of Tesserae, a 'meagre measure of grain and oil', is known to barely feed a citizen, and certainly does not provide ample nourishment. What's more, it's given only as part of an individual's trade with the government, a payment of one entry into the Hunger Games Reaping bowl in addition to their automatic one-entry per year, with entries accumulating year on year. The series holds a bleak outlook on hunger, and it is appropriate that these issues resonate in the real world, particularly for fans. What's more, the fans are engaging with these issues as active agents for change.

In an interview with Down With The Capitol, Adam Spunberg, host of the Hunger Games Fireside Chat podcast said that, 'Collins's trilogy has become an electrifying force for altruism – more than the other YA [young adult] fandoms – and, cheesy as this sounds, maybe people will leave hoping to make this world a better place.' The Hunger Games fandom recognizes its own force for good, and the Hunger Games name has been used to amplify social issues in the real world. From stories about 'The Real Hunger Games' taking place in North America to fans' attempts to co-opt Suzanne Collins's message in a greater campaign for social good, The Hunger Games has become an important reference point in both the political landscape and fan activism.

Fans and critics have compared Panem's 'bread and circuses' and economic inequality with the same issues in the real world. Let's look at Matthew Yglasias's piece published in Slate which dissects the economic circumstances of Panem. He compares the economics of Panem to historical patterns in the real world, pointing out that 'extractive institutions keep the entire District in a state of poverty despite availability of advanced technology in the Capitol'. The Government of Panem keeps its citizens on the breadline, carrying out work like mining and harvesting that could be more efficiently completed using its apparent technology. Forcing the lowest echelon of society below the breadline also has a knock-on effect on the local District economy. As Yglasias points out, in the case of coal miners in District 12, miners in the Seam are paid a subsistence wage by the Capitol government; but if it were to allow coal miners to earn more, the workers would spend money on more expensive staples or even luxuries. If this were allowed to happen, the Mellark Bakery, the apothecary, and other merchant services would also thrive, receiving greater custom. By keeping the Districts poor, the Capitol keeps its power. The entrenched monopoly of the Capitol government, like in the free market, also leads to a lack of innovation. As Panem District citizens come to know all too well, once established, these types of extractive institutions are very difficult to get rid of. Just as Katniss becomes a catalyst for change in The Hunger Games, leading to the revolution in Mockingjay, fans and campaigners alike have seen and understood

Fan Philosophies & Activism: *The HungerGames* for Social Good

this important message contained within the story and have begun to use it as their own catalyst for social good.

The Hunger Games has been used as a point of comparison for a number of campaigns, including a fight against cuts to US government assistance programs. On 8 May 2012, Melissa Boteach and Katie Wright – staff members on the Half in Ten campaign at the Center for American Progress Action Fund, which aims to reduce poverty by 50 per cent in the next ten years – wrote a guest post on *Think Progress* ahead of a controversial House of Representatives vote which threatened to cut over $33 billion from the Supplemental Nutrition Assistance Program (popularly known as the 'food stamps' programme).

In their report, Boteach and Wright referenced *The Hunger Games*, stating that:

*Fig. 1: Lionsgate, World Food Programme, and Feeding America teamed up for a campaign entitled* Ignite the Fight.

In *The Hunger Games*, the wealthy people of the Capitol leverage their power to create a game only they can win. Unfortunately, this is a storyline similar to one that many Americans know all too well. Lionsgate, the studio behind *The Hunger Games*, seemed to recognize that – they partnered with a number of anti-hunger charities as part of the movie's rollout, though they cracked down on other advocates who were riffing off the franchise's themes.

It's time to tell conservatives in Congress that we're done playing these hunger games. We don't need to cut food assistance for families struggling against hunger in order to finance more tax breaks for millionaires and to bolster our bloated military budget [...] Help us spread the word about these cuts – share our *Hunger Games* trailer and weigh in with your members of Congress now.

The campaign is entitled 'The Real Hunger Games', and its trailer intercuts movie footage with scenes of Congressman Paul Ryan introducing his budget proposals, statistics on food stamp usage, and stories from food stamp recipients. To date, the video has received over 44,000 views and is an upfront comparison between the politics of Panem and those of the US government. Despite their efforts, the $5 billion food stamps budget cut went into effect on 1 November 2013, affecting over 49 million Americans. The TYT Network posted a follow-up video on 11 November 2013 called 'The Real Hunger Games: Food Stamp Cuts Kick In, Causing Poor Families To Struggle More', which discussed the ways in which families have been adversely affected by the decision.

Lionsgate has its own charitable campaigns, too. In 2012 and 2013 the company partnered with Feeding America and the World Food Programme to drive donations. During the marketing campaign for *Catching Fire*, Lionsgate launched another campaign called Ignite the Fight (#ignitethefight), which transformed the *hungergames.com* homepage into a hub for exploring and sharing facts about hunger, and which allows users to donate to partner charities and register to win prizes. The page also allows fans to purchase exclusive merchandise, the proceeds of which benefit its partners. Lionsgate

Fig. 2: The Harry Potter Alliance (HPA)'s Imagine Better
project focussed on hunger.

also partnered with Subway, stating in a press release that, 'Lionsgate will utilize their promotion to support Feeding America, a non-profit organization consisting of more than 200 food banks nationwide.' These efforts redouble those from 2012, which fans had some other ideas to improve upon.

Fans have also used *The Hunger Games* in creative ways to mobilize activism campaigns for the greater good. Henry Jenkins has become the pre-eminent scholar on the subject of fandoms and fan activism, and has carried out research with support from the MacArthur and Spencer Foundations. He has explored the movement of fan activities as civic activities in detail, a movement that he calls transmedia activism. Online discussions and community sharing have become key ways to promote awareness-raising activities and to develop grassroots campaigns in favour of political and charitable causes. One fandom which has excelled in this arena over the past decade is the Harry Potter fandom. The Harry Potter Alliance (HPA) is a non-profit organization run primarily by Harry Potter fans, as well as members of other fandoms. It was founded by Andrew Slack in 2005 to draw attention to human rights violations in Sudan. Since then it has run a number of successful campaigns, many in partnership with other charitable causes, including Help Haiti Heal, which raised over $123,000 for Partners in Health in Haiti. HPA also teams up with fellow fandoms, like the Wizard Rock community and 'Nerdfighers' (nerds who fight 'to decrease world suck') – a fandom united by John and Hank Green or the 'vlogbrothers' on YouTube. Other HPA campaigns include Bullying Horcrux, fighting bullying with the Gay-Straight Alliance, and its annual books for kids drive, Accio Books.

The HPA also harnessed *The Hunger Games*'s message in the Imagine Better Project. In their own words:

The Imagine Better project takes a grassroots approach to harnessing the energy of popular culture, modern mythology and social media for social change. It is a place where we take all of the stories and communities that excite us and turn them into fuel for a better world. Where fans of all stories can join forces to turn the fictions they love into the world they can imagine.

In March 2012, the HPA teamed up with Oxfam International on the 'Hunger is Not a Game' campaign. The campaign involved raising awareness online using the hashtag #notagame in order to encourage sign-ups to the Oxfam GROW Pledge. One element of the campaign saw representatives circulating during midnight release parties for *The Hunger Games* film. The Oxfam pledge calls for simple reforms to food aid policy and procedures. On the *New York Times* 'Opinionator' column on 21 March 2013, contributor Courtney E. Martin stated that

It's worth paying attention to this campaign, not just because 'The Hunger Games' film is projected to make $90 million at this weekend's box office, but because Imagine Better is an example of how social change organizations are looking to tap into the extraordinary market power of Y.A. fiction – now the world's fastest growing literary genre.

Martin also quotes Andrew Slack, who says:

> There are a few key strategies that make fan activist campaigns like The Harry Potter Alliance successful: invest deeply in the literary themes, prize weirdness, honor the power of cohesive online communities and link to larger organizations that can implement the big ideas of plot-fueled real world advocacy.

Despite, or perhaps due to, this mainstream positive reinforcement of the HPA's project, Lionsgate responded, leading to what the *LA Times* referred to as a 'charity kerfuffle'. As *Think Progress* reported, Lionsgate's senior vice president for business affairs and litigation, Liat Cohen, issued a take-down notice to the campaign. The letter, reproduced in full on the *Think Progress* website, stated that Hunger is Not a Game was, 'piggy backing off of our motion picture "The Hunger Games"' and 'using Lionsgate's fans and fan Internet sites' to promote its cause, causing distortion of the film's title and 'causing damage to Lionsgate and our marketing efforts'. The letter pointed to Lionsgate's own efforts, partnerships with the UN's World Food Program and Feeding America, stating that, 'We are encouraging fans to support this effort by going to www.wfp.org/hungergames.' The letter also stated that Lionsgate was looking for an amicable solution and requested immediate removal of any mention of *The Hunger Games* from the campaign.

Andrew Slack e-mailed *Think Progress* features editor Alyssa Rosenberg thus:

> 'Fans have been changed by this story and have expressed a wish to change the world based on the message of this story,' Slack emailed me. 'I would hope that Lionsgate would celebrate fans, not pick on them, for taking the message of their own movie seriously. It's amazing that they're working with two great partners already to fight hunger. But why get in the way of fans who are working with a third one?'

In response to this news, a 26-year-old Hunger Games fan called Holly McCready created a *Change.org* petition. The page read, in part (original emphasis):

> Instead of treating us like an enemy, Lionsgate should embrace our heart and hard work. Advocating to feed the hungry and bring about a change should [be] celebrated. I know that together we can make a difference.
> The Hunger is Not a Game initiative has already given me the opportunity to act on the themes that moved me within the Hunger Games series, and I've already been

able to work [to] end poverty and hunger – and it's even gained the attention of The New York Times. Every fan should have the same opportunity.
Tell Lionsgate to stand with us, not against us.

The petition earned 18,618 supporters to date. Reportedly over 17,500 of these signatures were received within the first few days. This led to Lionsgate, as the *LA Times* put it, 'relenting' on the matter. At 6.12 p.m. on 23 March, Steven Zeitchik reported that, 'The spokeswoman added that the company did not intend to pursue further legal action against Imagine Better.' *Think Progress* also followed up, reporting that Lionsgate had 'reconsidered in the wake of widespread fan outrage'. Quoting her own correspondence with those involved, Alyssa Rosenberg writes:

> Kate Piliero, the vice president for corporate communications for Lionsgate's film division, emailed me to say that the company's main concern was that their official charitable partners for the film have exclusive use of the film's official images and logo (Imagine Better had created its own, separate set of images and branding) [...]
> In America, if not in Panem, it seems, fans and corporations can co-exist without a legal fight to the death.

The HPA has not reported on the results of the Hunger is Not a Game campaign. Since March 2012, though, the campaign has grown and changed. The HPA later began a new campaign along the same vein as a response to Lionsgate's own charitable efforts. 'Odds in Our Favor' uses the revolution of the Panem Districts in *Catching Fire* as inspiration for a plan to 'take back the narrative' about economic inequality. The campaign page reads:

> Economic inequality knows no boundaries – it is pervasive and persistent, and it affects every city, region, and country across the world. The gap between the wealthy and the poor grows wider every day, while the middle class shrinks and more people find themselves short of what they need to get by.

That the messages within *The Hunger Games* have been parlayed into campaigns for social good is testament to the writing of Suzanne Collins. In a promotional interview with ScholasticTeens the author was asked what she hoped young readers would take from The Hunger Games books, and she answered that she would want readers to think about whether they take their next meal for granted while others starve. Evidently this message has hit home for our current generation of online campaigners who Henry Jenkins calls 'netizens'.
It is clear that these young activists are inspired by the positive messages they find embedded in popular culture. But why is this the catalyst which sets their activities

Fan Philosophies & Activism: *The HungerGames* for Social Good

*Fig. 3: A fan-made logo in support of The Hunger Games and its message.*

alight? In an interview with *Le Vent Tourne in Ramallah*, a training blog on webfiction and transmedia, Henry Jenkins said that, 'Many young people, in particular, feel locked out of the language through which policy debates are held,' and that the language used is difficult to enter. Fan activists are creating a new language to ascribe the political process, mobilizing social communities, and integrating political participation into their everyday lifestyle. He also describes much of HPA's process of forging networks and creating partnerships, without displacing the current modes but creating their own in the process.

> The fan activists, then, are seeking to extend the capacity of these groups […] I am not suggesting that these approaches are an 'alternative' to traditional activism; they are rather an augmentation onto other mechanisms by which groups seek to publicize their concerns and mobilize their supporters.

Jenkins clearly believes that these agents for change often originate with young people in fandoms, but can extend well beyond that niche sphere of influence.

> Both the entertainment education and fan activist models have strong potential to foster greater public awareness and civic participation. They are addressing some of the limitations of politics as usual. They are reaching segments of the population who have not seen themselves as political agents before.
> Where these approaches work, it is because they are in the hands of communities and leaders who have a deep understanding of participatory culture, a deep commitment to their causes, and a serious appreciation of the value of the communities with which they are interacting.

Beyond fan activity specifically, many reporters have drawn parallels between the contents of *The Hunger Games* and zeitgeist issues – even those at the other end of the political spectrum. Steven Zeitchik of the *LA Times* asks if *The Hunger Games* movie is 'a cautionary tale about Big Government. And undeniably a Christian allegory about the importance of finding Jesus. Or maybe a call for campaign-finance reform?' He argues that *The Hunger Games* 'has become the rare piece of Hollywood entertainment: a canvas onto which disparate and even opposing ideologies are enthusiastically projected'. Zeitchik also points to a Fox News pundit who believes that *The Hunger Games* is 'a furious critique of our political system, in which the central government grows rich from the toil of the masses, even as that same political elite finds entertainment in the contrived and manipulated death of its subjects'. Meanwhile, 'The Real Hunger Games' was busy with its campaign, using the film's images and message in opposition to impending government cuts to aid programs.

Readings of *The Hunger Games* diverge hugely: while one news pundit unpacked a treatise on Big Government, fan activists were mobilized in support of the impoverished and hungry. While art and, indeed, *The Hunger Games* is open to interpretation, it is clear which readings inspire positive, active communities to campaign and thrive, bringing together communities for change which strive to help pull people out of hunger and into life's more cheerful games. For a further in-depth analysis of Suzanne Collins's messages, including hunger, in opposition to Lionsgate's marketing of *Catching Fire*, see Chapter 4. In Chapter 7, we'll look at some of the more playful ways in which fans interact with *The Hunger Games* and its message. ●

~~~~~~~~~~~

## GO FURTHER

### Online

'The Real Hunger Games: Food Stamp Cuts Kick In, Causing Poor Families To Struggle More'
*TYT Nation* [YouTube]
11 November 2013, http://www.youtube.com/watch?v=qnH8svCttPk.

'Press Release: "SUBWAY(R) Restaurants And Lionsgate Team Up For The Hunger Games: Catching Fire"'
*Wall Street Journal.* 8 July 2013,
http://online.wsj.com/article/PR-CO-20130708-906404.html.

'Lionsgate's Partnership with Subway: Fresh or Not Fresh?'
*Hunger Games Fireside Chat* [YouTube]
17 July 2013, http://www.youtube.com/watch?v=K3pakIOXER8.

'Interview with Henry Jenkins'
*Le Vent Tourne in Ramallah.* 27 December 2012,
http://training-cfi-le-vent-tourne-in-ramallah.com/2012/12/27/interview-with-henry-jenkins/.

'Guest Post: The Real Hunger Games'
Melissa Boteach and Katie Wright
*Think Progress.* 8 May 2012,
http://thinkprogress.org/alyssa/2012/05/08/480157/guest-post-the-real-hunger-games/.

Fan Philosophies & Activism: *The HungerGames* for Social Good

'The Real Hunger Games (Video)'
*ThinkProgressVideo* [YouTube]
8 May 2012, http://www.youtube.com/watch?v=zu3nGD7HxoO.

'Lionsgate Won't Shut Down 'Hunger Games'-Inspired Anti-Hunger Advocates'
Alyssa Rosenberg
*Think Progress*. 24 March 2012,
http://thinkprogress.org/alyssa/2012/03/24/451243/lionsgate-wont-shut-down-hun-ger-games-inspired-anti-hunger-advocates/.

'EXCLUSIVE: As "The Hunger Games" Opens Big, Lionsgate Tries to Shut Down Anti-Hunger Advocates'
Alyssa Rosenberg
*Think Progress*. 23 March 2012,
http://thinkprogress.org/alyssa/2012/03/23/450357/exclusive-as-the-hunger-games-opens-big-lionsgate-tries-to-shut-down-anti-hunger-advocates/.

'"Hunger Games": Lionsgate relents in charity kerfuffle'
Steven Zeithchik
*LA Times* '24 Frames'. 23 March 2012,
http://latimesblogs.latimes.com/movies/2012/03/hunger-games-petition-oxfam-let-ter-charity.html.

'Lionsgate: Don't Stop Hunger Games Fans From Fighting Hunger!'
Holly McCready
*Change.org*. March 2012,
http://www.change.org/petitions/lionsgate-don-t-stop-hunger-games-fans-from-fighting-hunger.

'From Young Adult Book Fans to Wizards of Change'
Courtney E. Martin
*New York Times* 'Opinionator'. 21 March 2012,
http://opinionator.blogs.nytimes.com/2012/03/21/from-young-adult-book-fans-to-wizards-of-change/?_r=0.

'Airtime Assault #35: Meet the Voices Behind the Hunger Games Fireside Chat'
*Down With The Capitol*. 17 June 2011,
http://hungergamesdwtc.net/2011/06/airtime-assault-35-meet-the-voices-behind-the-hunger-games-fireside-chat/.

'Economics of The Hunger Games'
Matthew Yglesias
*Slate*, 22 March 2012
http://www.slate.com/articles/technology/technology/2012/03/the_hunger_games_
could_a_real_country_have_an_economy_like_panem_s_.html

'How Harry Potter is inspiring muggles to help from Haiti to Darfur'
Gloria Goodale
*Christian Science Monitor*. 15 November 2010,
http://www.csmonitor.com/USA/Society/2010/1115/How-Harry-Potter-is-inspiring-
muggles-to-help-from-Haiti-to-Darfur/.

'Helping Haiti Heal'
*Harry Potter Alliance*. [n.d], http://thehpalliance.org/action/campaigns/helping-haiti-
heal/#sthash.2iSqOdBe.dpuf.

'The Imagine Better Project'
*Harry Potter Alliance*. http://thehpalliance.org/imagine-better/#sthash.47YniOmK.
dpuf.

'Odds in Our Favor'
*Harry Potter Alliance*. [n.d.], http://thehpalliance.org/action/campaigns/odds-in-our-
favor/.

'Suzanne Collins Answers Questions About The Hunger Games Trilogy'
*This is Teen* [YouTube]
2 September 2010, http://www.youtube.com/watch?v=FH15DI8ZW14.

# Fan Appreciation no.3
# Sara Gundell on Reporting on The Hunger Games

Sara Gundell is a specialist on The Hunger Games and has been reporting on the series at *The Hunger Games Examiner* since 2010. At the time of writing she has written well over a thousand posts about The Hunger Games. Sara has a BA in English and over ten years experience in print, online and TV news. She has a love of all-things Young Adult lit and runs the education-based YA (young adult) website *Novel Novice*. Sara has also written a graphic novel, *FAME: Suzanne Collins* (2012), which offers a look at how events in her life helped shape the series that would make her a household name.

**Nicola Balkind (NB):** When did you first pick up The Hunger Games books, and what drew you to the series?

**Sara Gundell (SG):** I first picked up *The Hunger Games* in early 2010, before *Mockingjay*'s title/cover had even been revealed. I had just launched my own YA book blog, *Novel Novice*, and was hearing lots of buzz about this book in the blog-o-sphere, so it seemed important that I check it out. I only bought the first book to begin with, but ended up racing out to my local B&N the morning after finishing *The Hunger Games* so I could get *Catching Fire*. Then the agonizing wait for *Mockingjay* began.

**NB:** Did you recognize something unique about the series? What made you want to stay involved with the fandom?

**SG:** I don't think there was anything in particular I could point to and say, 'That! That is why these books are so popular and great!' Overall, it was just this sense of the books connecting with so many people on such a broad basis. Suzanne Collins presents such a horrifying concept in these books, and yet they're not all that far removed from reality. It was captivating.

I definitely knew early on that this series was destined for a massive explosion in pop culture. Before *Mockingjay* was released, the series had the same sort of pre-burst energy I'd witnessed with Twilight (Stephenie Meyer, 2005-2008) before it hit the scene. I could tell it was going to become a cultural phenomenon in the same way, and that's actually what prompted me to start the 'Hunger Games Examiner' column.

**NB:** How did you first come to be involved in the Panem-verse/THG fandom?

**SG:** As I started to say above, I noticed this hum of activity surrounding

**Fan Appreciation no.3**
Sara Gundell

the series a few months before the publication of *Mockingjay*. Readers were agonizing over the wait for the last book, and news about the movie adaptation was starting to percolate. I was already a writer for *Examiner.com*, but I recognized the potential for The Hunger Games to be 'the next big thing' along the same vein as Twilight. That's when I pitched the column idea to *Examiner*, and they gave me the green light. (It's worth noting that coverage of YA series in general has increased exponentially on *Examiner.com*, now with its own hub: https://bitly.com/YAFicsandFlicks. The hub was spear-headed by Amanda Bell, who writes a variety of YA-related columns for *Examiner*, including Twilight, Divergent (Veronica Roth, 2011-2013) and YA fiction in general.)

**NB:** What do you think it is about THG that brings people together?

**SG:** The same thing that brings any fandom together – the mutual love of a book/series/TV show, etc. that resonates on a large scale with a diverse group of people.

**NB:** Do you have any experiences with in-person THG meet-ups?

**SG:** I don't – though I've been involved with in-person meet-ups for Twilight and for YA books in general, and they're pretty amazing. Most of my local friends aren't into YA lit, so it's really thrilling to get to hang out face-to-face with my 'Internet friends', with whom I share a passion for something as nerdy as books.

**NB:** Do you reread the series? If so, in your rereads, have you had any surprising changes in perspective? Anything you loved and grew to dislike or vice versa?

**SG:** I reread the first two books before *Mockingjay* was published, but that's it. Because I review and feature so many books for *novelnovice. com*, my reading schedule is pretty jam-packed, and I'm fairly rigid about sticking with it. Honestly, I have to be disciplined with it, or else I'd never get anything done for my blog.

**NB:** Where do you see the movie franchise going? Do you think the fandom has a long life beyond canon texts?

**SG:** I think the arc of The Hunger Games fandom will be similar to what we saw with Twilight. The popularity will continue to grow, the fandom will be categorized in the mainstream media in a particular way, hipsters will make fun of the series, and eventually the movies will end, and the frenzy will die down. As much as The Hunger Games is a huge part of pop culture right now, I'm not sure it has the same longevity as, say, the Harry Potter series (J.K. Rowling, 1997-2007) – which is a fandom that I think will always prosper and thrive. (But that's a whole other conversation ...)

**NB:** What have been your experiences with fan activism surrounding THG?

**SG:** I'm not sure I understand this question ... if you mean how fans act within the THG fandom, I've found it's much like any fandom. There are really hardcore, diehard fans out there ... and honestly, they frighten me a bit. They get so worked up over the littlest things, and as much as we may love something like THG, it's just not worth getting upset over something like Finnick's costume, or whether Delly Cartwright is left out of the movie or not. I wish I could just broadcast a message across the entire fandom: 'It's okay to be excited, but please keep things in perspective!' I think that's the danger of a fan's passion, when it gets out of control. It's that whole 'screaming teens' idea that was perpetuated by Twilight.

**Fan Appreciation no.3**
Sara Gundell

These fans *are* a minority (in any fandom), but they do exist and they tend to draw the most media attention because they have the most dramatic reactions and responses to whatever they are passionate about.

Also, I just have to say for the record, I get so sick of 'fandom wars', in which fans of one series will diss another series. I see a lot of Twilight hate from THG fans, and that really bothers me. (It goes beyond this, but this is the most common example). I hate this notion that because you're a fan of one series, you can't be a fan of another. I know other fansite admins feel the same way – especially since many of them run other websites for other fandoms! Most of us are just hugely passionate about YA books in general.

**NB:** Favourite book and scene, and why?

**SG:** *Mockingjay* is my favourite book of the series. I really love the way it wrapped up the series in a way that felt natural and honest, but wasn't as totally devastating as it could have been. I felt like there was a bittersweet but mostly happy ending, and it felt genuine. I know it's a source of contention amongst fans, but I particularly enjoyed the epilogue. I thought it really ended everything on a poignant note.

**NB:** What is it about a book, series or fandom that makes you want to report on or create new stories around it?

**SG:** If I love something, I want to share it with the world. That said, there are some negatives to reporting on a fandom – I'll address that in one of your later questions. And I'll be honest – I get paid to write for *Examiner*. Not a lot, but it is a job – and the effort I put into my articles wouldn't be worth it if I were doing the work for free.

**NB:** In what new and/or surprising ways have you or do you connect with other fans? Did you ever expect this fandom to become so huge?

**SG:** Mostly I connect with fans through my articles, and on social media. Twitter seems to be the most active for me, but I'm also on Facebook and Tumblr. Personally, I've loved getting to know (at least online) the admins of other THG fansites. They're some of my favourite people, ever.

I'm not surprised by the size of the fandom. As I mentioned earlier, I was anticipating this huge cultural explosion. I remember talking to a local TV news show a few years ago, when Twilight was really big, and predicting that The Hunger Games would be the next big thing. It's fun to brag about, that I called it.

**NB:** What have been some of your favourite stories to uncover or report on?

**SG:** Oh, gosh, honestly, they all start to blur together.

Actually, I do remember, before *The Hunger Games* movie was really into the casting process, I interviewed actress Jodelle Ferland about her interest in the role of Katniss. She's quite active on Twitter, and is a huge THG fan, so she was following me. She and I had a lovely Twitter conversation one day, which lead to the interview. It was really fun, and she's just a genuinely sweet, interesting young woman. I love Jennifer Lawrence's portrayal of Katniss, but I still think Jodelle could have done a wonderful job.

(The interview was posted on *The Hunger Games Examiner* in two parts – see the Go Further section for links.)

**NB:** What has been the personal and professional impact of combining your own fandom with writing and reporting?

**SG:** Here's my dirty secret: reporting on The Hunger Games has really disenchanted me as a fan. There are a number of reasons for this, of course. For one, it's no longer just a passion … now it's a job. So I can't just hear about some bit of news and be excited … I have to write and promote an article. Then there's the hassle of dealing with the bureaucracy of a major movie studio … for my own sake, I won't go into details, but let's just say I don't have any warm fuzzy feelings towards them. Plus, seeing how many promotional campaigns are rolled out, I can't get excited about them because I just see the gimmick for what it is: a gimmick. On top of all that, there are the extreme fans (I referred to them earlier) who, honestly, just get annoying. I have some sort of rebellious side that these uber-fans trigger in me, causing me to feel more negatively towards the series.

This doesn't mean I'm not still a fan. I am. I didn't get exuberantly excited when Lionsgate started teasing the *Catching Fire* trailer. But when I finally saw it? Yeah, it was pretty cool. But I have noticed my passion wane as a result of reporting on the series for so long. (It's been three years, man!)

**Fan Appreciation no.3**
Sara Gundell

~~~~~~~~~~

## GO FURTHER

**Books**

*FAME: Suzanne Collins*
Sara Gundell
(Vancouver, WA: Bluewater Productions, 2012)

**Online**

'Jodelle Ferland is a "Hunger Games" fan first, but would love a role in the film'
Sara Gundell
*The Hunger Games Examiner*
Part 1, 13 October 2010: http://www.examiner.com/article/jodelle-ferland-is-a-hunger-games-fan-first-but-would-love-a-role-the-film
Part 2, 14 October 2010: http://www.examiner.com/article/jodelle-ferland-talks-about-up-coming-projects-acting-at-such-a-young-age

**Websites**
*The Hunger Games Examiner*, http://www.examiner.com/the-hunger-games-in-national/sara-gundell
*Novel Novice*, http://www.novelnovice.com

# THE BIRD, THE PIN, THE SONG, THE BERRIES, THE WATCH, THE CRACKER, THE DRESS THAT BURST INTO FLAMES. I AM THE MOCKINGJAY. THE ONE THAT SURVIVED DESPITE THE CAPITOL'S PLANS. THE SYMBOL OF THE REBELLION.

**KATNISS EVERDEEN**
CATCHING FIRE

Chapter
7

# Playing at *The Hunger Games*: Fandom Play Online & IRL

→ The Hunger Games fan participation reaches far beyond reading the books, seeing the movies and discussing the texts with friends. Lionsgate has created immersive games which extend The Hunger Games story or recreate it in order to allow fans to participate in the shoes of their favourite characters. Creating and recreating the story is also common practice for members of the fandom.

Fans interact on forums and fan pages, often taking part in discussions of the books and films, but also delving into performative activities like role play. Fans have created their own spaces for role playing or interacting in-game with the world of Panem in various ways, including through writing, gaming, or in person.

### Hunger Gaming

Lionsgate, like many other film companies, created tie-in games with *The Hunger Games*. Its hugely popular Facebook game, 'The Hunger Games Adventures' (2012), has well over 100,000 players, and has also been ported to iOS to be played on handheld Apple devices. Its creator, a company called Funtactix, says it is 'redefining film-based gaming by giving fans the ability to have a deeper relationship with the worlds they love'. The game follows the same arc as the film, allowing fans to take part in the story for the duration of time between movie releases. Listed activities include hunting and trapping in the wilderness, trading in the Hob, visiting the Mellark Bakery, and discovering new parts of Panem throughout the gameplay experience. This rich content commissioned by the rights holders is both a gaming experience and a way to immerse oneself in the storyworld. From a marketing perspective, it also creates loyalty with the story, keeping fans in touch with official news and activity with social media updates as a tie-in.

Lionsgate's tie-in games also have some fun incidental links to the story's origins. Early reviews of *The Hunger Games* compared the story with two of Stephen King's novels, both of which he penned under the pseudonym Richard Bachman: *The Running Man*, (1982) in which the protagonist takes part in the titular game show wherein contestants are chased by 'Hunters' that are employed to kill them, and *The Long Walk* (1979), in which 100 boys compete in an annual walking contest held by a totalitarian government. Lionsgate has released two movie tie-in games. The first, *The Hunger Games: Girl on Fire* (2012) coincided with the release of *The Hunger Games* movie. It's described as a 'teaser' game, and has garnered reviews which agree that the game left them wanting more from the world of Panem. The second tie-in, commissioned by Reliance Games, is called *Panem Run* (2013). Like *The Long Walk* it is an endless-runner game; unlike *The Long Walk*, the goal for the player is to play a District member of Panem and spread hope through the Districts, collecting the sparks and materials that Katniss has left behind.

### Where gameplay and role play collide

Just as Suzanne Collins saw the blurring of truth and fiction while flipping between Iraq war news and reality television, the boundaries between gaming and role play can be quite malleable. While some fans, as we'll see in Chapter 9, continue the storyline or create stories of their own revolving around the series, many more extend this activity into the various ways in which they play online and in real life.

Transmedia storytelling can be a form of gaming, and alternate reality games (ARG)

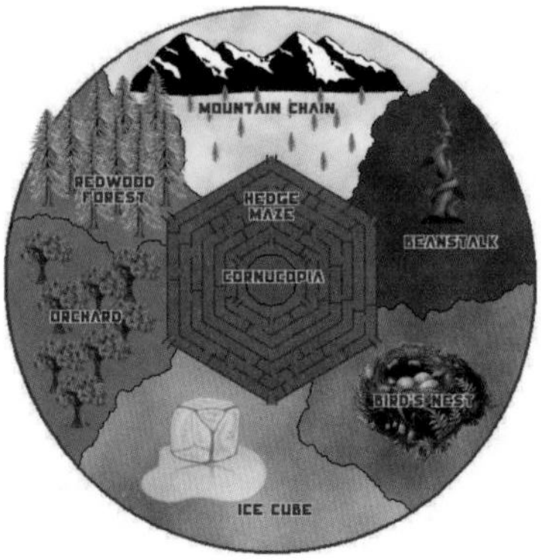

Fig. 1: *The Hunger Games RPG* made its own map for the Quarter Quell Arena.

– a type of transmedia storytelling – is a form of interactive networked narrative. These use the real world or, in this case, the Internet, as a platform to deliver a story. These transmedia stories usually take place across online spaces, a website, and associated social media accounts, and the plot may be altered by the actions or ideas of participants. ARGs like Lionsgate's website *The Capitol PN* (thecapitol.pn) allow participants to take part in the story of *The Hunger Games* online in this type of text-based environment. Users sign up and receive a District Identification Pass and District assignment, and thereafter they act as a Citizen of Panem, following instructions from the Capitol as they are passed down from on high. Twitter and Facebook pages support this activity, keeping players in the loop without having to visit the homepage. Activity is not simply centralized to the Capitol government, either – Twitter and Facebook profiles exist for every District. The concept of *The Capitol PN* is similar to that of a fan-created ARG called Panem October, which launched in October 2012 but which, after disagreements with Lionsgate, was subsequently shut down. (You can read all about Panem October in Chapter 8.) In ARGs, all messages are delivered as if in-universe. For example, Citizens are reminded to 'reserve your seats now' for 'mandatory participation' at the Quarter Quell, with a link to make an advance purchase for cinema tickets to see *Catching Fire* via Fandango. Transmedia activities like these allow for some fan role playing activity, but many more fans go far beyond these Lionsgate-provided spaces to create their own.

## Role play

Role playing, whether it's live-action role playing (LARP) or a role playing game (RPG), is a celebrated pastime in many fandoms. Be it Medieval warriors, teen wizards or Tributes, role playing of all kinds allows fans to partake in play in which they express themselves by becoming their favourite characters.

Role playing (commonly RP) has long been a popular practice online, allowing participants to inhabit their chosen character without make-up, dress, or other trappings. Fans of *The Hunger Games* take part in RP on various sites around the Internet, including at the *Hunger Games Roleplay Wiki*. This particular game takes place years after the events of the books, so you can't play Katniss or Peeta, but you can populate a world filled with new characters and take part in Reapings, and Hunger Games in any of the twelve Districts. Players fill in their profiles, including their name, District, age, gender, weapon of choice, and other aspects of their character. Another type of online RP is *The Hunger Games RPG*, a popular multiplayer role playing game based on the series that was launched by Dragonprime Development in March 2012. The website invites you to participate, stating that: 'Survival is key, determination is vital, and the odds ... May they be forever in your favor.'

While both of these role playing games take place in purpose-built, walled-garden websites like the above, other fans prefer an independent, freestyle role play. The blog-

Fig. 2: Cosplayers photo-
graphed at the base of Tripple
Falls, where The Hunger
Games was filmed.

ging platform Tumblr is rich with interactions of this kind, with individuals role playing as their favourite characters and improvising with each other. For example, one user called notsolittlepeeta, role playing as Peeta, participates in an exchange with another called flamingarcher, role playing as Katniss:

> Katniss: Katniss looked up at him and reste [sic] her chin on his chest and looked up at him. 'I don't remember falling asleep.' She told him. 'I sat down on the floor and woke on the sofa. I think Haymitch had something to do with it. I know he's home. I saw his light on and Hazelle was cleaning up like before the rebellion. I think he saw the medics escorting me in.' She explained and lowered her head again.
>
> Peeta: 'Eat some more and then we'll sleep for a while, okay? You need to rest well.' He knew she needed it and he knew that she'd be stubborn but he had to make sure that she got what she needed to be able to feel a little better than how she most likely had been feeling the past few days.

## Cosplay

Cosplay (a portmanteau of 'costume play') is a type of role play where fans craft elaborate costumes and dress as their favourite characters. Considered a performance art, this form of role play usually takes place at pop culture events like conventions or fandom meet-ups. In Chapter 5 on representations of race and disability, we see how a cosplayer named Pan was empowered and excited by the knowledge that Katniss was described as olive-skinned in The Hunger Games books, and how it allowed her to access and explore the possibility that a person of colour could become a powerful agent of change.

Outfits for the 74th Hunger Games are fairly easy to recreate with black or khaki trousers, boots, a tight-fitting T-shirt and a rain jacket. This coupled with a braid makes a Katniss, or with short blonde hair resembles Peeta. For this reason, cosplay for The Hunger Games is quite widespread at events like midnight screenings. One prominent YouTuber, Kate Elliot (Katers17 and katersoneseven), dressed up as Katniss in this manner for the midnight screening of The Hunger Games movie and in a parody video. For more adventurous cosplayers, Effie Trinket's big colourful hair and bright make-up is a popular choice – see DeviantArt users Mirish and Megan Coffey, as well as Mahogany who also features in Chapter 5. Many cosplayers hang out on DeviantArt and upload images of their costumes, hair and make-up at home and at events.

While some cosplay as their favourite characters from a single book, film, game or franchise, many more make a habit of cosplaying across genres and stories. Prominent Vancouver cosplay group Fighting Dreamers Productions has been cosplaying together since 2007 and, around the time of The Hunger Games movie release, took on Katniss and Peeta. They also filmed a series of video skits in-character, including 'Get to Know

Your Tributes' in which they combine the YouTube style of vlog-
ging with the story of the Capitol's pre-Games interviews and their
version of capture the flag.

## IRL play
Moving away from the role playing elements of the Hunger Games
fandom, let's take a look at the more literal aspects of 'play'. Character play can be fun and rewarding, but with a dark tale like *The
Hunger Games*, incorporating the overall story arc into real life can be a tricky business,
as demonstrated by the fact that some elements of Hunger Games IRL (in real life) play
have come under scrutiny within the fandom. For example, as discussed in Chapter 4,
negative fan reactions followed the announcement that Lionsgate were in talks to build
a Hunger Games theme park. Many fans cited troubling issues, including the violence
portrayed in the story and the representation of poverty of Panem's Districts as entertainment; both notions fly in the face of Suzanne Collins's intended message.

*Fig. 3: A fan's photo diary from IRL play with* Hunger Games *Official Fan Tours.*

However, like our fan activists in Chapter 6, many fans have taken The Hunger
Games out into the real world in a bid to get young people interested in the series. Back
in 2010, the National Council of Teachers of English threw an event based on the series at Colorado State University. Students partook in their own version of the Hunger
Games, which included a Cornucopia filled with 'weapons' like basketballs and water
balloons. Another story involved a summer camp in Largo, Florida, which became news
after its plans to run a Hunger Games-themed programme were revealed. The camp's
head counsellor, Lindsey Gillette, spoke to the *Tampa Bay Times*, saying that the violent
intent expressed by the kids was 'offputting', sparking a change of plan which refocused
their Hunger Games competition with a positive spin. The game included four worksta-
tions where the kids could test their intellect, balance and poise, and teamwork to gain
points. In the 'capture the flag'-style game that followed, children would 'collect lives'
or flags from their teammates, rather than 'killing' each other.

Other game adaptations have arisen to suit the themes of The Hunger Games. One
*wikiHow* page describes 'How to Play the Hunger Games Outdoor Game' which is an
elaborate version of 'tag'. With over 80,000 hits to date, its popularity suggests a real
desire for ways to play a version of the Hunger Games IRL. The goal of the game is to
remain the last person standing, and in this version, concessions have been made to the
players who are knocked out, allowing them to become sponsors of the game. While in-
appropriate for younger children, this is a great example of the influence of The Hunger
Games and a perceived desire to translate its rough-and-ready elements into in-person
gameplay.

## Literary & cinétourism
Fans also find new ways to interact with their favourite texts through place. For some

*Fig. 4: Amanda Bell from Next Movie mapped a fan road trip to The Hunger Games filming locations.*

fans this could mean set visits, visiting a theme park, creating their own version of a scene or, in the case of films like *The Hunger Games*, visiting the real-life places which stood in for Suzanne Collins's iconic locations in the films. Twilight (Stephenie Meyer, 2005-2008) fans flooded to Bella Swan's hometown of Forks, Washington, influencing an enormous rise in average annual visitors from 10,000 to over 73,000 within three years. Meanwhile the Lord of the Rings trilogy (Peter Jackson, 2001-2003), shot in New Zealand, has been widely reported to have turned landmarks like Mount Ngauruhoe – which served as Mount Doom in the movies – into tourist destinations. Literary- and ciné-tourism is booming for *The Hunger Games*, too, and for scenes from the first film there's a one-stop shop in the state of North Carolina, where the first movie was shot in its entirety.

The small, abandoned Henry Mill River Village stood in for District 12 locations including the Seam, the Everdeen home, and Mellark Bakery, while nearby town Shelby became the town square for the iconic Reaping scene. In Charlotte, 45 miles to the east, the James L. Knight Theater became the set for the interview scenes in which Caesar Flickerman introduces Katniss and Peeta to their soon-to-be adoring Capitol audience. Moving on to the Games itself, DuPont State Forest was the filming location for the majority of the Arena action, with the healing, nourishing yet perilous water served by North Carolina's natural treasures including Triple Falls, Little River and Bridal Veil Falls. Movie locations for District 12 and the 74th Annual Hunger Games Arena are hugely popular with fans, many of whom take the pilgrimage to seek out the real places used to depict the world of Panem on film. Many more take it a step further and recreate the experience altogether.

Competing fan tours offer a unique, partially performative, experience to Hunger Games fans, providing immersive tours which incorporate storytelling and challenges to immerse fans in the world of the Arena. Jeff Coffey of Asheville, NC started *thehungertours.com*, an unofficial tour company offering seven Hunger Games-related expeditions. Whether fans fancy a four-to-six-hour hike on the Cave or Survival Tours, prefer to kick back and see the city sights on the Capitol Tour, or even see it all over the course of two days, these tours have welcomed fans from 37 states and 6 countries.

Meanwhile *Hunger Games Unofficial Fan Tours* (hungergamesunofficialfantours. com) offers similar day tours at DuPont State Forest in the Blue Ridge Mountains of North Carolina's Transylvania County and Henry River Mill Village in Burke County, around 60 miles from Charlotte. The company also runs an Adventure Weekend inspired by scenes and events in *The Hunger Games*. Participants check in to their lodgings at Earthshine Discovery Center, eat foods inspired by *The Hunger Games* movie and books, and are provided with a day of guides, survival classes and night-time zip lining followed by an all-day, all-out survival game.

These are great examples of fans travelling to the point of origin to re-enact events from the series, learning to take part in archery and survival skills, and getting the 'ulti-

Fig. 5: The Mellark Bakery in
Henry River Mill Village and
on-screen.

mate immersive experience' – as authentic an experience as possible. The company's tours are also following the film-makers to Atlanta where plans are being made to expand and run a *Catching Fire* locations tour. Although in-depth records of the tours from fans are thin on the ground, the company's Facebook page is a trove of enthusiastic thanks, Instagram photos and related events for North Carolina natives and cinétourists alike.

Fan play encourages personal identification with the story and the spaces which it inhabits. These forms of play take place in pre-created spaces like video games, trans-media storytelling online, and in person. All of the above dimensions allow fans to take the place of their literary heroes either as part of the story in-game, through their own expressive writing, or physically as part of a performance. Many more also like to visit the places where the story was conceived or performed in the movie itself, bringing them a little bit closer to the narrative and providing a place and time over which to bond with their favourite texts or, for fans, friends and family, with each other. Many more forms of fan creation are born out of play, as we will explore further in Chapter 9 on fan creation. ●

## GO FURTHER

*Games*
*The Hunger Games Adventures*, http://www.thehungergamesadventures.com/.
*The Hunger Games Adventures* [Facebook], https://www.facebook.com/TheHungerGamesAdventures.
*The Hunger Games: Girl on Fire*, https://itunes.apple.com/us/app/hunger-games-girl-on-fire/id512146822?mt=8.
*Panem Run*, https://itunes.apple.com/gb/app/hunger-games-catching-fire/id723466333?mt=8
https://play.google.com/store/apps/details?id=com.reliancegames.hgpanemrun&hl=en_GB.
*Hunger Games Roleplay Wiki*, http://hgrp.wikia.com/wiki/Hunger_Games_Roleplay_Wiki.

*Articles*
'Tie-in mobile game for The Hunger Games: Catching Fire is a competitive endless-runner'
Chris Priestman
*Pocket Gamer*. 12 November 2013,
http://www.pocketgamer.co.uk/r/Android/The+Hunger+Games%3A+Catching+Fire+-+Panem+Run/news.asp?c=55213.

'How to Play the Hunger Games Outdoor Game'
Various authors
*wikiHow*, http://www.wikihow.com/Play-the-Hunger-Games-Outdoor-Game.

'Movies in the Mountains'
Cara Ellen Modisett
*Blue Ridge Country*. 1 July 2012,
http://blueridgecountry.com/newsstand/magazine/movies-in-the-mountains/.

'"The Hunger Games" Travel Guide'
Amanda Bell
*Next Movie*. 25 April 2012,
http://www.nextmovie.com/blog/hunger-games-travel-guide/.

'New literary tourism: read it, watch it, live it'
Harriet McLeod
*Reuters*. 22 April 2012,
http://www.reuters.com/article/2012/04/23/us-usa-tourism-books-idUSBRE83L0AQ20120423.

'The Hunger Games tour: See the sites of District 12 and more'
Sarah MacWhirter
*The Globe and Mail*. 4 April 2012,
http://www.theglobeandmail.com/life/travel/destinations/the-hunger-games-tour-see-the-sites-of-district-12-and-more/article4098063/?page=all.

*Role play*
*Not So Little Peeta* [Peeta role player], http://notsolittlepeeta.tumblr.com/
*Flaming Archer* [Katniss role player], http://flamingarcher.tumblr.com
*Fanfiction.net* 'Hunger Games Roleplay', http://www.fanfiction.net/forum/The-Hunger-Games-RolePlay/101913/
*Confessions of Hunger Games RPers*, http://confessionsofahungergamesrpers.tumblr.com/
*The Hunger Games RP*, http://thehungergamesrpforumotion.tumblr.com/

*Cosplay*
Mirish as Effie Trinkett: http://mirish.deviantart.com/art/May-the-odds-be-ever-in-your-favor-292119822
Megan Coffey as Effie Trinkett: http://megancoffey.deviantart.com/art/Effie-Trinket-Tea-Time-297780411

Katersoneseven as Katniss: http://www.youtube.com/watch?v=jVzEELww-k0
Katers17 Hunger Games Bloopers Parody: http://www.youtube.com/
watch?v=yJA2BWOvy9E
Fighting Dreamers Productions as Katniss and Peeta:
http://www.youtube.com/watch?v=B0E1RibPAFM
Fighting Dreamers Productions: A Hunger Games Exclusive:
http://www.youtube.com/watch?v=6sNWodHcZW8

*IRL play*
Colorado State University's Hunger Games:
http://www.youtube.com/watch?v=pJdp_O4OsLs

'At "Hunger Games" camp, children want to fight to the "death"'
Lisa Gartner
*Tampa Bay Times*. 2 August 2013,
http://www.tampabay.com/news/humaninterest/at-hunger-games-camp-children-
want-to-fight-to-the-death/2134621.

*Literary & cinétourism*
North Carolina Tours and Adventures for Fans of 'The Hunger Games':
http://gosoutheast.about.com/od/northcarolinatravel/ss/north-carolina-tours-and-
adventures-for-fans-of-the-hunger-games.htm.
*Hunger Games Unofficial Fan Tours*, http://hungergamesunofficialfantours.com/
*The Hunger Tours*, http://www.thehungertours.com/

# SO, NOW THAT WE'RE DEAD, WHAT'S OUR NEXT MOVE?

**GALE HAWTHORNE**
MOCKINGJAY

Chapter
8

## The Fans vs The Man: The Capitol PN vs Panem October

→ Early in the days of The Hunger Games's popularity, before Lionsgate purchased the rights to make the movie adaptations, there were the early seeds of a fandom growing online. Fansites began to spring up, and among the early adopters, some of them are still the biggest online gathering hubs for Hunger Games fans, including Mockingjay.net, TheHungerGamesTrilogy.net, The Hob, Down With The Capitol, HG Girl on Fire, and the Hunger Games Fireside Chat podcast.

Fig. 1: A screenshot from Panem October during its heyday.

But amidst the typical fansites filled with news and chat, one website popped up in April 2011 with an interactive approach. *Panem October* sought to become the biggest and best ARG (alternate reality game) based around *The Hunger Games*. Alternate reality games are networked narratives which take place in realtime. Participants interact directly with the characters in-game, and the story evolves based on their actions and responses. ARGs are now more commonly known as transmedia storytelling devices, and mainstream publishers and media companies are making an effort to appeal to fans through these means. The key to success for a transmedia campaign as a marketing platform is to create long-term engagement with products. *Pottermore*, the ARG based around the Harry Potter series (J.K. Rowling, 1997-2007), is a successful example of the form. However, when fans are first up to bat with this kind of activity, it can get up the marketing department's nose. One website who learned this the hard way was *Panem October*.

*Panem October* was a hub aimed at fans of The Hunger Games series, creating an experience for fans, by fans. The webmaster, going by the moniker Gamemaker Rowan, had originally pitched the idea to Lionsgate to no interest, which sealed its position as a fan-driven website. Gamemaker Rowan's true identity has not been revealed, but he has said in interviews that he is a prominent member of another fandom and has been involved in other interactive fan websites. As Rowan told *Movies.com*, with *Panem October*, 'Our overall goal is to provide an unforgettable experience for the fans as they await the release of the Hunger Games film.' The full experience was set to launch on 1 October 2011, six months before the 23 March 2013 premiere of *The Hunger Games* movie and the beginning of its very own Hunger Games storyline.

Initially, two URLs directed to the website: *welcometopanem.com* and *hungergamestesserae.com*. A Twitter account called *@PanemGovernment* dispensed tweets to fans, often in a malevolent manner. In a review of the website, on 3 October 2011, fansite *Welcome to District 12* said:

Finally, October is here and we have gotten the first glimpse of the Panem October experience. It's very impressive for a fan-made ARG. There's still so much left of it [to] uncover, yet there's a great deal you can do: friend each other, leave a Panem-oriented Facebook-like status, Panem Radio, and keep racking up scans of your Panem ID to reveal your district's website. Even with all this, there are still new features to be readily available and more parts of the website to uncover. Panem October is setting an extremely high bar.

## The Fans vs The Man: The Capitol PN vs Panem October

*Fig. 2: The Panem October welcome page.*

Continuing with their pre-launch strategy, *Panem October* began sign-ups, teasing Panem ID cards featuring QR codes. Users would be sorted into Districts, then could use the QR code to access special areas of the website. A collaboration between fansites took place, with the sites taking turns presenting ID cards for key characters. In webring style, each site also interlinked between each of the other fan sites taking part, telling readers which character could be found where. For example, President Snow was released on *Down With The Capitol*, while Effie premiered at *The Hunger Games Examiner*, Peeta appeared on *Mockingjay.net*, and our heroine Katniss's ID card was first seen on *Movies.com*.

Everything seemed to be going well for *Panem October* – until 6 November 2011, when the Gamemakers received a letter from the legal department at Lionsgate. Gamemaker Rowan told the full story in an in-character interview with *Down With The Capitol*:

> We approached the company your people refer to as 'Lionsgate' back in April, detailing our plans to bring Panem to you. Follow-ups were attempted on our end here in Panem, but we seemed to be stringing along with no progress. In June, we were surprisingly contacted by Lionsgate and were asked to take down both hungergamestesserae.com and welcometopanem.com, along with the removal of digital artwork that belonged to Lionsgate. They believed the websites to be a scam, attempting to collect user data. We explained the mistake of the situation and that apparently the right departments were not speaking to each other. We gave names of those we were in touch with at Lionsgate to clear ourselves and obliged with their takedown requests. We then attempted to make real contact after the incident, numerous times, and repeatedly hit dead ends.
>
> We strongly believe that if fansites and fan-created content like artwork, websites and games are allowed to happen, then we should be to [sic]. Games like ours only help the brand, create loyalty in the fans, and quite honestly they get them more excited and enthusiastic about sharing the series with more people (or 'customers', where necessary). What we're doing is incredible and beneficial to both Lionsgate and Scholastic. I'm glad to see Lionsgate bringing fan-created productions into the spotlight, such as their 'fan of the week' and their weekly promotion of the HG Fireside Chats. We are in the same boat as other fan-created productions. We are not charging users or selling their information. We are just very, very technologically-gifted fans who are taking hours from every day to create something for not only you, but ourselves, the fans. Because of this belief, we have respected their requests, and have moved everything to panemoctober.com (and have given a better disclaimer and method of contact, for sure).

Soon after this activity, Lionsgate began its own efforts with a website called *The Capitol PN* (thecapitol.pn), an interactive game with a similar focus. In *Panem October*, the

DISTRICT 8 IDENTIFICATION PASS

NICOLA BALKIND

DATE OF BIRTH
03-19-1988    GENDER
              GIRL

MIGRATED FROM
GLASGOW

COUNTRY
UNITED KINGDOM

ASSIGNED OCCUPATION
WAREHOUSE MANAGER

PANEM CITIZEN NUMBER (PCN)
PN7HM9.1CH8AG

8
TEXTILES

*Fig. 3: Author Nicola's District ID pass from The Capitol PN.*

aim of the game was to follow the Hunger Games canon, inserting the user into the experience of the story in real-time, rather than creating any new, non-canon stories or character arcs. As Gamemaker Rowan put it: 'We will put the fans into the books themselves and make them feel as if they were living in Panem while the Hunger Games are happening.' The sudden appearance of *The Capitol PN* seemed to be timed with the legal letters to *Panem October*, sparking off a number of blog posts on the topic in the Hunger Games blogosphere. A website called *sullenandhostile.com* reported that there was a silent battle between *Panem October* and *The Capitol PN* for a time. Shortly after the launch, *Panem October*'s servers crashed, at which point, it seems, *The Capitol PN* made a surge in activity. Several commentators have claimed that Lionsgate and its digital agencies actively copied ideas from the *Panem October* announcements and developments.

In his resignation letter, which was sent to *Panem October* members on 15 December 2011, Gamemaker Rowan recounted the events of October thus:

> The first month and a half of PO was going swimmingly, and according to plan [...] and then TheCapitol.PN (Lionsgate) began increasing their activity and began executing their ARG as well. While PO activity was constantly evolving and happening, PN began to be more active, too. After a while, it became quite clear that PN's goals and objectives were very, very similar to PO's. Sometimes it was blatantly obvious that PN was carbon-copying social media or game-based moves, sometimes a mere hour (sometimes less) after the same PO postings. This doesn't come as a shock. Lionsgate, Sony and Scholastic employees were some of many watching over Panem October. One can argue their ARG has been in planning and was only now coming into play, but I know competition when I see it.

*The Capitol PN* emerged as a canon transmedia story featuring gameplay in the run-up to the release of the film in March 2012. Much like *Panem October* and, indeed, *Pottermore*, users sign up and receive a District Identification Pass and begin to explore the world of Panem. *The Capitol PN* was teased at the MTV Music Awards on 29 August 2011, followed by the appearance of Facebook and Twitter accounts for individual Districts, and processing of District ID passes began on 30 September 2011. On 3 October, Hunger Games fansite *Welcome to District 12* compared the websites, and concluded that Lionsgate seemed to be upping their game due to the presence of *Panem October*. Two days later, the fansite posted a blog filled with screengrabs of the newly designed and relaunched *Panem October* and reviewed the sites side-by-side, giving an outsider's perspective on events:

> The fact that Lionsgate allowed these two to exist is a godsend. It really showed me

that they actually do care about what fans want. I love that not only is Panem October allowed to flourish, but Lionsgate is making efforts to keep their ARG up to par. If not for Panem October launching, would TheCapitol.PN have started assigning recruiters as soon as they did? I'm not too sure, but it really seems that because Panem October exists, TheCapitol.PN is stepping up their game.

Much of the *Capitol PN* campaign was run by an agency called This Moment, which was hailed in a 2012 article by John Furrier, author of the Forbes blog *Silicon Angle*. The article entitled 'How a Startup Powered Hunger Games into a Global Social Phenomenon' calls the Hunger Games marketing campaign a 'money machine'. This came shortly after the movie's release, and cites how the film broke Fandango pre-sale records with 1,200 sold-out screenings. This Moment CEO Vince Broady is quoted as saying that the 'new approach is to leverage dynamic customer input instead of the old style of phased, programatic marketing campaigns'. In simpler terms, This Moment began its marketing programme for Lionsgate in summer 2011, seeking the audience's interest and active participation in the story long before the product launch – or, in this case, the movie release date. Early social media promotions included user-submitted videos as well as a set of videos with cast thank-yous to the fans: extras that fansites like *Panem October* would probably never have access to.

This type of fandom-focused marketing in opposition to fan-driven sites could be well on its way towards a huge cultural movement. Sean Kleefield writes a column on *MTV Geek News* called 'Fanthropology', which looks at fandoms from Star Trek (Gene Roddenberry, 1966) to The Hunger Games, identifying areas in which fandoms become equal and can be examined as a single entity. In the column 'Fandom as Big Data' he looks at possibilities for targeted marketing. In one example, he outlines how Mountain Dew's fan base is interested in snowboarding and what this means for their targeted marketing. The problem for big companies is that there is too much data to find key correlations. (For example, ideally Lionsgate would be able to identify a fan who has watched the *Catching Fire* trailer, bought tickets to San Diego Comic Con, and made an order for a fan-made Mockingjay pin from Etsy.) The article is a fantastic summation of how fandoms are viewed from the other side. When corporations own many of the characters that fans love, they are, to an extent, controlling the message. Fan passion is viewed and calculated by the rights owners as numbers and statistics: how many T-shirts sold, tickets purchased, and so on. Fan culture activities like fanfiction and other fan creations serve as an antidote to this cold measurement, and fandoms flourish with unauthorized activity. However, this also means that fans have unwittingly encroached upon sanctioned activity. *Panem October* caught the attention of the fans, many of whom assumed it was a Lionsgate property, so Lionsgate came to see the enterprise as a threat. The result was a cease and desist order, which ultimately limited free and open fan activity online. As Kleefield says in another column about cosplay ('#20: Cosplay-

Fig. 4: The District 12 Facebook sign-up order from The Capitol PN.

ers'), 'While the fans take it upon themselves to interpret and reinvent the stories according to their own interests and needs, it's still up to the companies who own the properties to choose how they look at and engage with these makers.'

The *Capitol PN* campaigns demonstrate this control of the message, which we explored from another angle in Chapter 4, 'Propos: The Publicity vs The Message'. Lionsgate has also undertaken an 'engage and ye shall receive' style approach to marketing. For example, upon signing up for *The Capitol PN*, users were encouraged to tweet using topical hashtags like #wheresmydistrict and #headforthesquare. Much like the Capitol of the films, it demanded 100 status shares before the *Capitol Tour* would open for registration, whereupon users could guess the password to the closed website using clues scattered around the web.

To claim their district uniform, users were to use the hashtag #lookyourbest, and community managers were selected on Facebook, where *The Capitol PN* requested citizens show their District loyalty, encouraging 'model' citizens to e-mail and enter into District Mayoral elections. Soon after this call to action, twelve users were selected as 'Recruiters' – community managers who were early adopters and that Lionsgate and its marketing agencies had apparently identified as leaders. Internet newspaper *The Daily Dot* reported on the story, interviewing some of the new Recruiters, all of whom were big fans and were spending huge amounts of their free time on community management for the website.

With all of this big spending and the official campaign's ability to call upon its massive audience, *The Capitol PN* rose above the fan-created *Panem October* which was run by a handful of loyal users, edging them out with the rise of a juggernaut which gained momentum towards the movie's bonanza opening weekend. But what were Lionsgate afraid of in these relatively small fansites? Were they concerned about the possibility of a groundswell of support towards this fan-driven activity, or being accused of copying the little guy? Lionsgate has not been explicit about its motives, but pushing *Panem October* to close forced the fandom to give up its own game in favour of Lionsgate's – which, one assumes, will help to earn Lionsgate more fans, more online activity, more brand loyalty and, ultimately, more money.

Historically, mainstream media companies like publishing houses and film distributors have not excelled at relationships with fandoms. As described in Melissa Anelli's fantastic *Harry: A History* (2008), young fans of the Harry Potter book series were in for a nasty shock when Warner Bros. took the reigns of the Harry Potter movie franchise and sent 'cease and desist' letters to small fan websites, many of them child hobbyists. Lionsgate has been comparatively temperate, but the example of *Panem October* is part of the same kind of movement against fans and in favour of a more commodified, marketing-heavy approach towards community-building around popular, big-budget mainstream media properties.

Ultimately, Lionsgate's Goliath won, while Gamemaker Rowan moved on to other

### The Fans vs The Man: The Capitol PN vs Panem October

projects. Incidentally, his venture sounds quite similar to *Pottermore*. From his resignation letter:

> When I started this project, Lionsgate wasn't at all supportive. Repeated phone calls and emails went unanswered, ignored and worst of all I was shoved aside. After their initial request to take the website down (although I was in friendly discussion with them for two months), I brought it back as a different, more obviously-branded 'fan-powered' website […]
>
> I think the combination of feeling like TheCapitol.PN was constantly nipping at my heels, mixed with the inability to code two entirely-massive websites, ultimately led to the decision of leaving Panem October ('abandoning' is a more honest word, here).
>
> I feel bad for letting down the fans. I wish I had more time, more resources, and quite honestly the prep-time that should have went more into building the ARG. Fans (and fansites) were the ones responsible for making this such a highly-anticipated experience for fans, and I cannot express how sorry I am for being the one responsible for it not reaching its conclusion.

On 15 December, a *Down With the Capitol* reader commented:

> I can't help but be suspicious of Lionsgate's plan to release the puzzle poster today. I mean, there is a huge chance of it being a coincidence (100 days and all that), but I feel so sorry that Panem October's closing will probably be overridden by the poster frenzy. I will say I am truly sad and disappointed to see PO go; I've met great friends through the site, and remember that hilarious HG Fireside Chat episode featuring PO? A thank-you-so-much to Rowan for all the diligent work he pitched in for our fandom!

But it was not until March 2012 that the *Panem October* webpage changed to read, 'Panem October is no longer active. love you guys. maybe we'll do something in the future.' The script included a link to *fireiscatching.com* – but sadly, nothing has come of it.

Today, *panemoctober.com* is a closed, unregistered domain while *The Capitol PN* prevails. Now that the Quarter Quell is upon us, the arena has changed for fans with technological aptitude who want to take on *The Capitol*. Despite this incident, as we'll see in Chapter 9, fan creation is booming. ●

~~~~~~~~~

## GO FURTHER

**Books**

*Harry: A History*
Melissa Anelli
(New York: Pocket Books, 2008)

**Online**

'How A Startup Powered Hunger Games Into A Global Social Phenomenon – A Money Machine'
John Furrier
*Forbes.* 25 March 2012,
http://www.forbes.com/sites/siliconangle/2012/03/25/how-a-startup-powered-hunger-games-into-a-global-social-phenomenon-a-money-machine/.

Kleefeld's 'Fanthropology' #8: Fandom As Big Data
Sean Kleefield
MTV Geek. 3 May 2013,
http://geek-news.mtv.com/2013/05/03/kleefelds-fanthropology-8-fandom-as-big-data/

Kleefeld's Fanthropology #20: Makers Vs Consumers At San Diego Comic-Con
Sean Kleefield
MTV Geek. 26 July 2013,
http://geek-news.mtv.com/2013/07/26/kleefelds-fanthropology-20-makers-vs-consumers-at-san-diego-comic-con/

'Panem October Comes to an End'
*The Hob.* 15 December 2011,
http://www.thehob.org/2011/12/panem-october-comes-to-an-end.html.

'Volunteers run Hunger Games viral marketing campaign'
Lauren Rae Orsini
*The Daily Dot.* 18 November 2011,
http://www.dailydot.com/entertainment/hunger-games-viral-marketing-campaign/.

'How to Use Panem October'
*jojothemodern* [Tumblr]

The Fans vs The Man: The Capitol PN vs Panem October

18 October 2011, http://jojothemodern.tumblr.com/post/11470906145/how-to-use-panem-october.

'PanemOctober Re-Visioned and Re-Launched!'
*Down With the Capitol*. 5 October 2011,
http://hungergamesdwtc.net/2011/10/panemoctober-re-visioned-and-re-launched/.

'"The Hunger Games" viral site TheCapitol.pn – brilliant or boring?'
Andrew Sims
*Hypable*. 3 October 2011,
http://www.hypable.com/2011/10/03/the-hunger-games-viral-site-thecapitol-pn-brilliant-or-boring/.

'Panem October Vs. The Capitol.PN'
Courtney Custodio
*Welcome to District 12*. 3 October 2011,
http://www.welcometodistrict12.com/2011/10/panem-october-vs-capitolpn.html.

'#26 Fireside Chat: Meet the Gamemaker'
*Hunger Games Fireside Chat*. 26 September 2011,
http://www.hgfiresidechat.com/podcast/2011/09/26-fireside-chat/.

'"The Hunger Games" Countdown: Panem October Is Coming!'
Perri Nemiroff
*Movies.com*. 21 September 2011,
http://www.movies.com/movie-news/the-hunger-games-panem/4594.

'EXCLUSIVE: The Panem October Gamemakers Are Back!'
*Down With the Capitol*. 4 August 2011,
http://hungergamesdwtc.net/2011/08/exclusive-the-panem-october-gamemakers-are-back/.

'"Hunger Games" Viral Game TheCapitol.pn Explained'
Amanda Bell
*Next Movie*. 11 January 2011,
http://www.nextmovie.com/blog/hunger-games-viral-game-thecapitol-pn/.

*Lionsgate sites for fans*
*The Capitol PN*, http://thecapitol.pn
The Inaugural Capitol Tour [Facebook], https://www.facebook.com/media/set/?set=a.2

09438459158423.34312.117405415028395&type=3

*Fansites*
*Panem October*, http://panemoctober.com
*Mockingjay.net*, http://mockingjay.net/
*The Hob*, http://www.thehob.org/
*Down With The Capitol*, http://hungergamesdwtc.net/
*HG Girl on Fire*, http://www.hggirlonfire.com/
*Hunger Games Fireside Chat*, http://www.hgfiresidechat.com/
*TheHungerGamesTrilogy.net* is no longer active

# Fan Appreciation no.4
# Samantha Sisson & Aaron Darcy on Panem Kitchen

Samantha Sisson and Aaron Darcy are Hunger Games fans and the creators of *Panem Kitchen* – a fansite that explores the world of The Hunger Games through its cuisine. The website, launched in August 2013, was featured as Fan of the Week on the official Lionsgate page. Samantha is a textile designer and Aaron works as a graphic and web designer; both are avid cooks and also contribute to the fansite *Panem Propaganda*.

**Nicola Balkind (NB):** First of all, can you tell me about what you guys do?

**Aaron Darcy (AD):** My background is in design. That's my full-time job: graphic and web design. So that's where my role in this particular project is, design and looking after the back-end of the website.

**Samantha Sisson (SS):** Actually my background has nothing to do with cooking or the Internet! I have a background in fashion design and menswear. I work now as a textile designer.

**NB:** How did you first discover The Hunger Games?

**SS:** Only last year, actually. Just before the films came out I got in contact with a friend of mine from high school and she suggested I read the books because she said I'd like this whole fandom. So I decided to give them a try and obviously she was right. I just got totally sucked in as the movie came out.

**AD:** I first discovered it through Samantha. She was talking about it for a long time and eventually just gave me the books and said, 'You need to read this.' We actually read them again, together.

**NB:** Did you immediately start visiting fan websites?

**AD:** I personally didn't. I only really got involved with it around the time we started to talk about *Panem Kitchen*.

**SS:** No … the biggest thing I was involved with before this was DeviantArt. I'd posted a couple of things I'd drawn there. I followed a couple of the fansites but didn't really get too entrenched in those – they had some really hardcore fans on there … [laughs] and there are some that can be quite hard to swallow, I guess.

**Fan Appreciation no.4**
Samantha Sisson & Aaron Darcy

**NB:** You've since worked with *Panem Propaganda*. When did you discover them?

**SS:** Actually, when I first got into The Hunger Games I'd looked for a map of the country because I was interested in what people thought it looked like, and their map was one of the first things I found. At the time they just had propaganda posters and stuff, they weren't exactly a fansite yet. It was more like a type of fanart. We didn't get in contact with them until around June or July [2013]. Molly does post a lot of news and stuff but their content is in-universe, which sets it apart from everything else.

**NB:** How did you get involved?

**SS:** I drew a little comic of Johanna Mason's hair based on a conversation that Aaron and I had, and Molly happened to see it and she freaked out and said, 'I have to get you to draw for the site!' and 'You have to work on the site with me!' so that was it, I guess. I just got very lucky!

**NB:** So did *Panem Kitchen* grow out of that?

**SS:** We're kind of affiliates, *Panem Kitchen* is a separate entity. We started it. We actually came up with the idea way earlier this year.

**AD:** Yeah, maybe March of this year. The way we work together is very much feast or famine. We have a ton of ideas but only a few get completed. It's usually a slow process – so while the initial idea was in March, we only really started to work on it in mid-July. We really just knuckled down to get it finished, and getting the recipes together was about three or four weeks, maybe?

**NB:** Do you have any specific goals with *Panem Kitchen*?

**SS:** Well the idea was wanting to do something that expanded on the universe within The Hunger Games. Aaron called me one day and I said, 'Aaron, I love cooking, and I love The Hunger Games. Why have I never thought to combine them?' We thought, well, yeah, there were places who had done the recipes from the book – anything mentioning lamb stew and cheese buns and such – but we wanted to do something a bit different. So we said, what would be eaten in the Districts? Because each District would be focused in a region of the United States and they would

Cheese buns from the Mellark Bakery

all have their own recipes and culture through food and what's available to them. Also with this comes this movement in America to get back to simpler methods of cooking or living in general – and it seemed like the right time to put these two ideas together.

Since then we've done a couple of recipes from the book because you ask fans, 'What do you want to see us make next?' and of course they're like, 'Lamb stew!' So we ended up not being able to avoid that. But it's really fun to sit and brainstorm, like, OK District 6 is transportation, what District 6-specific foods are there?

**AD:** I think that's the aspect I enjoy most, getting to fill in the blanks that aren't in the book. A lot of it is just interpretation, like where a place is located within the former United States, but with this we get to expand on what we think these things could be.

**NB:** So how do you feel about something like fanfiction where a fan changes the storyline in their own way?

**AD:** Personally, I like to keep the storyline the same and fill in the parts that aren't mentioned. Fanfiction is fun and it's different, but one thing that we would never do is try to rewrite the book, or the story, or the characters. In fact we do the opposite: we like to take a character who we know is from a certain District and build upon what we know, then try to work that into our interpretation.

**NB:** Speaking of which, Samantha I loved your portraits with the accompanying stories.

**SS:** Thank you! Yeah, it's kind of like what Aaron said: that's something I'm keen to be working on because I can come up with my own backgrounds but I try to keep it as canon as possible. People that take it in a completely different direction are one thing and they have their own audience, but ... I guess I'm a Hunger Games purist!

**NB:** Was there anything particular in the books that made you want to delve in further?

**SS:** That's a tough question. I get really attached to characters, and the characters that Suzanne Collins created were what I latched on to most. So I had started on fanart and fanfiction based on those characters, and since then it's become more all-encompassing. But I think there was just so much open for interpretation with some of the characters that I wanted to fill in the blanks myself.

**NB:** Have you gone back and reread the books, and did rereading them change your perspective?

**SS:** I've read the series four times now, and each time I'll find something different, like some new foreshadowing or something about a certain character that I'd never noticed before. So there's always something new to notice and think about. And each time I read the story the message and the dramatic moments and the character relationships and all of that all come crashing back to me again and I'm always weeping over my Kindle!

**NB:** Do you have a favourite book in the series?

**SS:** My favourite is *Catching Fire.* A bunch of my favourite characters are introduced in it and I feel like the plot really gets rolling at that point.

**AD:** I would agree, I think *Catching Fire* is my favourite. I wish I could, like Samantha, point to a specific reason but I can't – it's just my favourite one.

**NB:** Interesting! *Catching Fire* was my favourite the first time around, too! When I reread them, though, I think *The Hunger Games* became my favourite. Is there a particular aspect of the story you have bonded over?

**AD:** I don't think there's anything in particular ... I'll probably regret saying that now ...

**SS:** Probably the relationship between Finnick and Annie.

**AD:** How did I miss that?

**SS:** How *did* you miss that? A couple of things in our lives parallel what they went through and so ... I can't speak for Aaron but they're very treasured characters for me.

**AD:** Yeah, they are, it's true. Even though it's not touched on in any great detail, again, we've filled in a lot of the blanks ourselves and that's how we relate so well to those two – a lot more so than Peeta and Katniss or Katniss and Gale. We see how Finnick is with Annie and how Annie is with Finnick and we can relate to that.

**NB:** Do you think people who are entrenched in the fandom tend to identify more with the secondary characters more than with the main three or four?

**SS:** I think you're kind of right because [...] how can I put this without sounding like a bitch? Casual fans can look at the main characters and see, oh dramatic love triangle! Two handsome men and a reluctant heroine! I feel like we have a lot of friends in the fandom now and all of them have favourite characters who aren't of the main three or four. Yeah, I can't think of a single friend of mine who'd pick Katniss or Peeta or Gale as their absolute favourite character. That is a weird trend.

**Fan Appreciation no.4**
Samantha Sisson & Aaron Darcy

**NB:** Why do you think that is?

**SS:** I think Katniss and Peeta and Gale serve such specific roles that they're all easy to relate to. But characters like Cinna or even Prim – I think they're the characters that people find more of themselves in.

**NB:** What has been the impact of your fandom activity on your daily lives?

**AD:** It's the first big project we have completed, so that's been a gateway to other things that we have in the works. We know we can plan for something and have it happen, which is good on a personal level. It has also introduced us to a lot of people within the fandom. The people at *Panem Propaganda* are probably the best example, they've been a great help to us, and we share a lot of ideas and insights. It opens up a door and it's fun to see the reactions of readers to the site who have something positive to say. We get a lot of really good feedback and also some genuinely good suggestions.

**SS:** I think we've gotten a lot out of it personally. We've definitely met a lot of great people and we've made a lot of connections with fans. Also, personally, it's so great to have something to work on together that we're both passionate about, and it's really fun to have a creative outlet that has to do with something we both love.

**AD:** We also get some good food out of it! [laughter]

**NB:** What about professionally?

**AD:** Not as of yet, but I wouldn't necessarily expect it – at the end of the day it's a fansite, it's not visited by anyone who's looking for design work specifically. I've had great feedback from readers, but no commissions as such. Over time we're going to continue to build the audience and tie it together with other projects so we'll see how that works out. It will certainly be added to the portfolio.

**SS:** We also have a lot of Hunger Games-related things coming up and we'll probably connect those with *Panem Kitchen* as well. But it is great to know that we can really pull something together, and seeing the success of *Panem Kitchen* has given me so much confidence in the other things we're planning.

**NB:** I noticed a District 4 theme – is that a Finnick and Annie connection?

**SS:** It is, yes! That's my personal preference. I can't help it.

**AD:** It is down to that, but there's also a practical point of view – District 4's industry is fish and there are any amount of fish and fresh fruits we could do. District 6's specialty is transport and that's all we know, so unless it's going to be a cup of coffee we don't know how to associate that.

**NB:** Have you been to any meet-ups in person?

**SS:** I don't know what opportunities there would be [where we live] – granted we've never really looked.

**AD:** It's interesting you mention that actually because it's not something we ever really notice. I'm sure it's the kind of thing that happens but, being as immersed in the fandom as we are, we've never really noticed it.

**SS:** Last year they tried to get a convention started but I think it was woefully underfunded and hadn't come together in the way they had hoped it would. It was entirely fan-driven. It was called the Victory Tour. I think they ended up doing an entirely online thing, but it was still very expensive to attend as I recall.

**NB:** What online kind of feedback have you had for *Panem Kitchen*?

**SS:** A lot of people have told us they're planning to use our recipes for *Catching Fire* parties. The recognition from Lionsgate – that was a biggie. Especially because the site felt very small at the time so it felt good to impress somebody!

**AD:** The nature of something like this is, we get 99.9 per cent positive comments, so although that is a good thing, you seem to already remember the bad comments. But we do owe an awful lot to being the Fan of the Week – there was a huge spike in awareness there. It was enough to make us open a Facebook account, which is really something, we both hate Facebook!

**SS:** We do get a lot of requests: make a grilled squirrel!

**Fan Appreciation no.4**
Samantha Sisson & Aaron Darcy

**AD:** We actually live deep in the woods and there are squirrels around so I am tempted to do a grilled squirrel and say, well, you asked for it! [laughter]

**NB:** That reminds me about the maps – did you do a lot of research on those?

**SS:** The map we have in mind is based loosely on *Panem Propaganda*'s but our Districts would be a lot smaller. So many maps have them as big as several states, and considering the nature of Panem and its government we don't really see it that way. I would see them all as the size of a large city at most.

**AD:** We think it will help to have a visual reference for the Districts and where they would be. We will make our own and publish it but there does seem to be an over-saturation of people's maps.

**NB:** That makes sense for the Districts to be smaller, especially with Reapings, etc. taking place in the town square – which wouldn't work in a state the size of Texas.

**SS:** Exactly. Somewhere they've got these 75 Arenas preserved as tourist destinations, but if you've got all the Districts butting up against each other, where are the Arenas?

**NB:** There must be a lot of empty space.

**AD:** Some maps show District 12 as a large portion of the East Coast, but if the population is around 8,000, we think they are tiny, cordoned-off areas then, as you say, a lot of dead space in the middle.

**SS:** Plus there's the fact that they're all separated from each other so that there's no contact between the Districts and so on.

**NB:** You've also now included recipes for the Capitol. What do you think of *Capitol Couture* and the current direction of the marketing?

**AD:** We kind of disagree on that.

**SS:** I think it reached a breaking point when they started marketing thousand-dollar tracksuits to fans. It feels like they've lost sight of the original message of the Hunger Games. They're making a big spectacle of it. It's just gotten … too Capitol. The marketing was really clever in the beginning, really exciting, it was fun to see everything in the universe. But then when they translated it into actual products [etc.], it just comes across as missing the point. They're thinking we're enamoured with the wrong side. I know there's a lot more happening that's exciting in the Capitol than in the Districts, but we're interested in the heroes, not the bad guys! Aaron's laughing at me.

**AD:** Where our opinions differ slightly is that I think that *is* the point, to market ridiculously priced clothing under the guise of the Capitol. I don't think [the thousand-dollar tracksuit is] there to generate income, I think it's there to generate publicity.

**SS:** I would love to think that! I would love to think that you're right and it's a marketing scheme, like 'Look! It's a big trick, we got you! You're the Capitol after all'. There has been fan backlash against it too, a lot of the fansites took issue with it.

**NB:** And do you think they're avoiding reporting on that?

**SS:** Um, some of them are. Some of them are avoiding that aspect and only report news now. I think they tolerated the *Capitol Couture* stuff to a point but eventually dropped it.

**NB:** Do you think casual fans are interested in it?

**SS:** From the feedback that I've seen, no. I think a lot of people are put off by it. It's cool to look at, it's neat to see that I could buy a training suit from *Catching Fire* … that no one can afford. Maybe that's the point!

**AD:** I think that the fans' backlash is about the message of the book. But I don't see it that way, I still see it as being under the *Capitol Couture* 'brand', if you can call it that. You're not supposed to miss the message of the book, you're supposed to look at it as the Capitol behaving exactly like the Capitol. It could be either one – I wouldn't be surprised either way, because we're dealing with a company who know this huge potential for marketing, so they're going to pull all kinds of tricks.

**Fan Appreciation no.4**
Samantha Sisson & Aaron Darcy

~~~~~~~~~~

## GO FURTHER

### Books

*Catching Fire Cookbook: Experience The Hunger Games Trilogy with Unofficial Recipes Inspired by Catching Fire*
Rockridge University Press
(Berkeley: Rockridge University Press, 2013)

*The Unofficial Recipes of The Hunger Games: 187 Recipes Inspired by The Hunger Games, Catching Fire, and Mockingjay*
Rockridge University Press
(Berkeley: Rockridge University Press, 2012)

*The Unofficial Hunger Games Cookbook: From Lamb Stew to 'Groosling': More than 150 Recipes Inspired by The Hunger Games Trilogy: From Lamb Stew to 'Groosling'*
Emily Ansara Baines
(Blue Ash: Adams Media, 2011)

*Catching Fire Cookbook: Experience The Hunger Games Trilogy with Unofficial Recipes Inspired by Catching Fire*
Rockridge University Press
(Berkeley: Rockridge University Press, 2013)

### Online

Websites
Panem Kitchen, http://panemkitchen.com
Panem Propaganda, http://panempropaganda.com
Capitol Couture, http://capitolcouture.pn
Samantha's Tumblr: http://65thvictor.tumblr.com/
Samantha on Panem Propaganda: http://www.panempropaganda.com/news/author/cresta

IT WAS MY ARROW, AIMED
AT THE CHINK IN THE FORCE
FIELD SURROUNDING THE
ARENA, THAT BROUGHT
ON THIS FIRESTORM OF
RETRIBUTION. THAT SENT
THE WHOLE COUNTRY OF
PANEM INTO CHAOS.

**KATNISS EVERDEEN**
MOCKINGJAY

# Chapter
## 9

# Consumption Becomes Production: Fan Creations and *The Hunger Games*

→ 'Consumption becomes production; reading becomes writing; spectator culture becomes participatory culture.'
Henry Jenkins, *Fans, Bloggers, and Gamers*

Cultural participation and the creation of fanworks have a long tradition in the world of fandom. Interaction with texts and franchises, particularly those with the level of cultural relevance of The Hunger Games series, often continue for many years beyond the creation of books and movies. Fandoms surrounding modern cult classics still foster active online fan communities who reread and rewatch, attend fan conventions and create their own stories around the original works that they love. One activity that is common to dedicated fans of many series is the creation of fanworks like fanfiction texts, fan videos and fanart. The writing and reading of fanfiction can begin early in the life of a cultural product and long outlast its popular interest. Fans began writing fanworks based on Suzanne Collins's *The Hunger Games* almost immediately after the books were published and, judging by the current fervour with which fanworks are being created, may continue for years to come.

Fanfiction is a fan-created text based on any canon creation which reworks, recreates, or reimagines the source material. Fanfiction writers are often known as 'ficcers', their work 'fics', 'fanfic' or even 'FF'. According to transmedia expert Henry Jenkins, fanfiction 'can be seen as an unauthorized expansion of these media franchises into new directions which reflect the reader's desire to "fill in the gaps" they have discovered in the commercially produced material' ('Transmedia Storytelling 101'). Indeed fans take varied approaches to fanfiction: some adhere strictly to the canonical fictional universe as created by the original author, while others stray, borrow from other fictional universes, or even invent characters whole cloth. Crossover stories are also a possibility where, for example, Harry Potter (J.K. Rowling, 1997-2007) characters may show up in the Hunger Games universe. 'Shipping refers to the activity of pairing particular characters into a relationship ('ship) that does not necessarily appear in the canon text and is also common practice, particularly in the creation of fanfiction. (Those which are canonically true may be called a 'sailed ship'.) In anime and manga-based fan cultures, "shipping' is more commonly referred to as 'pairing', hence the term OTP, or One True Pairing – but we'll get into this in more detail later.

The practice of writing fanfiction has roots in fanzines from fandoms like Star Trekkers of the 1960s and early Doctor Who (Sydney Newman, 1963) fans (or 'Whovians'). Nowadays, particularly for fans of The Hunger Games, fanworks are most commonly published online and receive rapid feedback from fellow fans, readers, and reader-creators. Fanfiction commonly appears on websites like *fanfiction.net*, *Wattpad*, *Movellas*, *Figment*, *AO3* and *Archive of our Own*. Fan videos may follow a similar format, though we'll see the diversity between forms at work throughout this chapter. Fan video works tend to appear on the ever-popular online video giant YouTube. Meanwhile creators of fan artwork often host their work on DeviantArt and share stills across social networking sites – specifically the fandom treasure trove (and most popular social network for 16–24-year-olds) known as Tumblr.

In this age of mass participatory culture, publishers and other rights holders hold

Consumption Becomes Production:
Fan Creations and *The Hunger Games*

various views on fan creation and inhabit different stances on the legality and accept-ability of fanworks. In *Textual Poachers*, Henry Jenkins divides these into three distinct groups: 'prohibitionists', who shut down unauthorized participation; 'collaborationists', who try to win grassroots creators to their side; and 'consumers', who want creators to participate only on the rights holder's own terms, dictating where and when the rights holders wish them to do so. Scholastic, the publishers of The Hunger Games series in the United States, owns messageboards where young fans are encouraged to post fanfiction for the entertainment of their peers. While Lionsgate has been connected with shutting down some fan participation activities, like the creation of online games (see Chapter 8 on the fan-made Hunger Games ARG, *Panem October*), they also foster community activity through activities like their Fan of the Week feature on the official 'The Hunger Games' Facebook page. As Jenkins also pointed out many years later (in *Convergence Culture*), 'Everyone involved – industry and audience alike – believes our culture will become more participatory but there is uncertainty about the terms of our participation.'

Regardless of terms, fan creation is booming. Until recently, fanworks like fics had long been considered subculture activities. However, the practice has reached main-stream consciousness with the help of the astronomical success of E. L. James's 50 Shades of Grey trilogy (E.L. James, 2011-2012), which began life as Twilight fanfiction, and the implementation of Amazon's Kindle Worlds programme, which it calls 'a place for you to publish fan fiction inspired by popular books, shows, movies, comics, music, and games'.

Within five short years, the Hunger Games fandom has proved itself to be as prolific as some of the world's most enduring fandom cultures. Its cultural relevance and hype have also played into the ubiquity of fan-created works from parody trailers to remakes to alternate universe fanfiction and 'shipping. Fan videos are highly visible, though less frequently perceived as transformative because audiences are used to seeing videos which recreate and parody pop cultural phenomena. Two of YouTube's most popular pop culture parody channels, Honest Trailers and Bad Lip Reading, have sent up *The Hunger Games* and *Catching Fire*; a channel called Teens React has dedicated two epi-sodes to the series; and Top 100 YouTubers like Joey Graceffa have created videos both honouring the series and incorporating its themes into pop music parodies with music videos. However, just as mainstream television culture is no longer top-down, feeding the masses what's popular, the same is true for online. The Hunger Games has been so hugely popular and widely parodied that we must seek to make a distinction between those video makers who ape popular culture and those who create a fan-oriented re-sponse to the original work.

Those with the skill and resources to make videos like Bad Lip Reading reap the most views, but many more fans are putting themselves through great pains of time and ef-fort to produce fanworks worthy of real reverence. We'll also look at fan-oriented pro-

*Fig. 1: Mainstay Productions creates Fan Videos based on The Hunger Games.*

*Fig. 2: The Online Musical recreated The Hunger Games using TY Beanie Babies.*

ductions like *Mainstay Pro* and *The Katniss Chronicles*, which see fans partake in the creation of professional-level transformative works.

### Canon & in-universe creations
*Recreations*
Regardless of the form, ficcers of all types tend to have a predilection towards one type of story over another. As mentioned above, some prefer to fill in the gaps, build upon, or extrapolate out a story from a clue bedded within the larger plot. Meanwhile others will invent relationships, imagined futures, and myriad other non-canon creations. Regardless of preference, fanworks are a further opportunity for engagement with both the Hunger Games universe and the self.

Numerous fan groups have attempted to recreate *The Hunger Games* in all sorts of weird and wonderful ways, from recreating and spoofing key scenes to filming music videos. One recent parody saw *The Hunger Games* play out as an 8-bit game. Another recreates the entire plot of *The Hunger Games*, portrayed by TY Beanie Babies, in little

## Consumption Becomes Production:
## Fan Creations and *The Hunger Games*

over 12 minutes, and still manages to capture the essence of the story. 'The Beanie Baby Hunger Games' is an irreverent take on the story created by a group called The Online Musical. The protagonist, Katniss Everbean, follows the same trajectory as the original, employing expositional dialogue and lines from the book to speed the plot along. The video has been featured in *Flavorwire*, *The Huffington Post* and *Mashable*. Though it purports to be a parody, there are gentler moments amidst the melodrama which suggest that its creators are fans of the series.

*The Katniss Chronicles* is a unique adaptation of The Hunger Games amongst fan creations which both adapts and expands upon the source story. In its own words, 'The Katniss Chronicles is an unofficial and unauthorized audio drama based on the bestselling book series The Hunger Games' and the website invites you to 'experience the story of the Girl on Fire, episode by episode'. This serialized, radio-play format bridges the possibilities of text and film, allowing its makers to take time over plot points, key and otherwise, and really develop its characters. It is a mostly textual adaptation, taking what is known and adapting it to the new medium. It also includes some extratextual material, creations beyond the literary source text which expand on moments informed by the mood of the piece. For example, most of Suzanne Collins's speaking characters appear, and some characters have also been created to illustrate plot points outside of Katniss's perspective. In Episode 1 an extratextual element debuts in the form of a pair of Capitol TV hosts named Bett Botlee and Angela Berliner, who introduce listeners to their Reapings broadcast. Much of the action and dialogue in *The Katniss Chronicles* is taken directly, or close to directly, from the source text, and segments throughout each episode are told from Katniss's perspective in voice-over. The series excels in its asides which highlight the vapidity of the Capitol characters, adding an extra element of cultural commentary to its reinforcement of Collins's message. In the scenes following Katniss and Peeta's triumph at the Games, Katniss's media literacy is addressed throughout her responses to what is happening around her. She understands that the footage of her floral tribute to Rue has been cut from the highlights reel because it signals rebellion, and she further explicates her understanding of Haymitch's orders to act like she is madly in love with Peeta as her only defence. The dramatization also succeeds at key points where audio allows them to show, not tell, what characters are feeling, and often this is achieved through sound effects and music as well as dialogue. *The Katniss Chronicles* features music by Sam Cushion, a prominent fan of The Hunger Games series and regular panelist on the *Hunger Games Fireside Chat* podcast. Sam is a musician who has created his own score for *The Hunger Games* and his score provides an atmospheric backdrop to the audio series.

In his study of Star Trek (Gene Roddenberry, 1966) fans in *Textual Poachers*, Henry Jenkins cited David Bleich's findings that male fans tended to be concerned with plot accuracy and the actions of a central protagonist, while female fans generally saw the narrative as if it were an 'atmosphere of experience' and enjoyed applying their own

Fig. 3: Fan art of Johanna
Mason from the website
Panem Propaganda.

inferences, emotions and knowledge to the storyworld. Whether this holds true today is up for debate; however, the responses that fans describe having to a piece of source fiction can be a great indicator of their depth of reading, and Sam describes his musical response to *The Hunger Games* as being primarily emotionally driven. In an interview with fansite *Down With The Capitol*, Sam Cushion said,

> The Hunger Games is filled with such powerful emotions on paper that I felt needed to be expressed in some way through music. I know the movie will be great but I wanted to write a score for the book. I have always been a fan of movie scores and I thought 'What's keeping us fans from making our own score for the books we love?' So I made one.

Sam also takes the emotions of other readers into account while interpreting his feelings to music. He adds that,

> The most challenging part of composing is trying to interpret all these emotions from the book in a way that most people can relate to. Even though you are reading the exact same words, the brilliant thing about books is the role your imagination plays. People interpret those words differently in the scenes that form in their minds. Trying to capture that with music can be a scary task sometimes.

In the same manner as professional composers of movie scores, Sam selected his favourite scenes, characters, places and events: 'I will just sit down and pick one out and write a song about the feeling I had towards that character or scene while reading,' he told *Down With The Capitol*. 'I like to give the main characters, or characters that stood out to me, their own theme. From there I can incorporate their theme into the major scenes that they are in.' This process is similar to that of professional composers working on movie scores, and has certainly served *The Katniss Chronicles* well. The reverence that *The Katniss Chronicles* cast and crew holds for the series demonstrates the power of their deep readings and expands on the story through their interpretations. Beyond adaptation and recreation, many fans have also found ways to create further news and comment in-universe and in-character.

### Embracing the extratextual

The fansite *Panem Propaganda* provides two kinds of news. The first is your typical fan-oriented news page, reporting on year-round developments like castings and red carpet coverage; but the second, the site's true focus, is extratextual: an in-universe take on the happenings of Panem. In a similar vein to Lionsgate's website *The Capitol PN, Panem Propaganda* publishes stories which are written as if passed down from the Capitol and its propaganda machine. One contributor has satisfied an urge to play Effie Trinket in

Consumption Becomes Production:
Fan Creations and *The Hunger Games*

an advice column, 'Dear Effie'. Another by the name of Martina Chekov (aka Samantha Sisson, creator of *Panem Kitchen*, see Fan Appreciation no. 4) has created Celebrate Your Victors, a series of Tribute portraits accompanied by a biography of each character. These use Suzanne Collins's descriptions as the primary text and expand upon them from the Capitol voice. For example, Johanna Mason's profile reads:

> Johanna has since enjoyed enduring popularity in the Capitol. Her biting wit and dry speech are her trademark, and there are those who actively antagonize her just to be the receptor of one of her wonderfully quick comebacks. While we doubt that Johanna will try to pretend innocence again in the Quarter Quell, we'd certainly be wary of her ability to deceive.

Fanfiction sites are filled with in-universe fics which adhere to canon but play with the form in different ways, primarily by extratextual means. One fic writer, Miss Scarlett 05 on *fanfiction.net*, loved The Hunger Games trilogy so much that she continued the story herself. 'Grow Together' follows on from *Mockingjay*, filling the timeline gap between Katniss and Peeta's return home to District 12 and Collins's epilogue. Many more fic authors have created similar challenges for themselves, spinning out new narratives which follow Katniss and Peeta or other characters after their canon challenges.

Similarly, many fan artists are adept at selecting meaningful moments from the source text and imagining them for their own purposes. A fan artist who goes by the Tumblr user name alonglineofbread creates and even commissions fanart pieces based on The Hunger Games. This artist demonstrates great skill in capturing emotion and brings to life kisses and cuddles between Katniss and Peeta, tender moments between them and their child, and moments from other fanfic texts. Many more of this artist's works are largely canonical. One remarkable example illustrates, over four panels, Katniss and Peeta's heartbreaking reunion in *Mockingjay*. First Katniss sees Peeta as Finnick and Annie embrace behind her, then a reverse shot image of Peeta sees him sitting on the hospital bed, regarding Katniss. In the third panel, Katniss runs towards him, tears streaming down her face, then in the fourth, we see Peeta's unexpected attack as he lunges for Katniss. This collaboration of sorts came from an idea by a fellow fan called Branchan (on Tumblr), who in turn commissioned the artist.

*Fig. 4-7:* alonglineofbread *on Tumblr recreates Katniss and Peeta's reunion in* Mockingjay.

Another fan by the name of LaurasMuse on DeviantArt took a key description from the books to create a one-panel image of Katniss's inventory at the beginning of *Mockingjay*.

She writes:

> I highly enjoyed Mockingjay and thought it was significant that Katniss kept an inventory of her belongings at different points in the novel. They include: the hunting jacket, the family plant book (turned to the page for the katniss plant, illustrated by Peeta), her parents' wedding picture, a silver parachute, the locket with pictures of Gale, Prim and Mrs. Everdeen, the Mockingjay pin, the spile and the pearl. All these souvenirs are great symbols for the series and what's great is that they all mean something to Katniss and help her get through an extremely dark time.

While the above examples create a visual interpretation of a scene in the book, some fan-video makers have deftly and expertly recreated moments which are mentioned in the books but do not feature in the thrust of the plot. Mainstay Pro is a production company which specializes in online video and has produced several stories from The Hunger Games series which are referenced but not necessarily expounded upon. Free from constraints over audience suitability, these are pitched at an older audience than Lionsgate's movies, and convey violence and brutality as well as a tremendous sense of pathos. 'The Hanging Tree' follows Katniss on her first hunting trip with her father, where he explains the evils of the Capitol and begins to teach Katniss to hunt. This is a direct interpretation of all of the key lessons which Katniss tells the reader that her father taught her, including how to detect whether the District 12 fence is electrified and the history of Mockingjays. Another video entitled 'The Second Quarter Quell' expounds upon the development of Haymitch and Maysilee Donner's relationship in the 50th Hunger Games, following the plot that Katniss describes in *Catching Fire* while preparing for the third Quarter Quell. Maysilee and Haymitch were allies during the Games, and Maysilee's token was the Mockingjay pin, which was passed down to her niece, Madge Undersee, and in turn gifted to Katniss. Maysilee was also close friends with Katniss's mother. There are many more fan theories surrounding Madge's mother (Maysilee's twin) and her morphling addiction. Many parts of this story have the potential to be unfolded as fanworks, and Mainstay Pro has recreated these canonical, fill-in-the-gaps episodes in professional fashion. Another series by the same company tells the story of Finnick and Annie's relationship – a romance between two of the series' most intriguing Victors.

Many more fics follow, in some cases even mimic, the source plot as far as possible but incorporate one or two major tweaks. One of the most-read fics on *Wattpad* is 'The Hunger Games' by Kaylene or Ienagurrrl, Part One of a retelling of the entire series. The fic has garnered well over a million views and Kaylene's version of events begins with the Reaping in District 12. The piece is narrated by Prim and follows an alternate storyline in which Katniss does not volunteer as Tribute in Prim's place. In a message embedded at the bottom of Chapter 3, the author writes, 'Like I said, this is my version,

Consumption Becomes Production:
Fan Creations and *The Hunger Games*

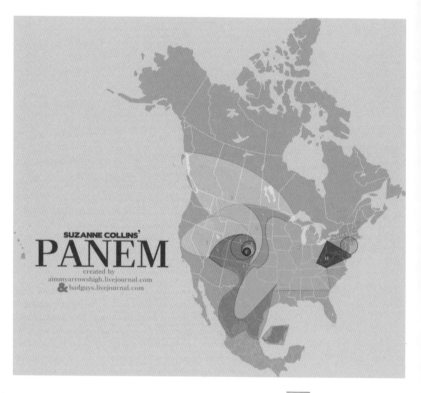

so alot [*sic*] of the parts are the same as the real book, but some parts are made up [...] it's kinda hard to write withOUT copying stuff from the original book.' Kaylene continues to follow major plot points, including the hand-holding in the Tribute parade, switching out the Katniss–Peeta romance in favour of a brother–sister bond.

*Fig. 8: V. Arrow and a fellow fan created their own theoretical map of Panem.*

## On exceptional readings

The brother–sister-bond element relates to a theory within the fandom which suggests that Primrose may be the daughter of Katniss's mother and Peeta's father. As Henry Jenkins writes in *Textual Poachers*, 'Fandom celebrates not exceptional texts but exceptional readings (though its interpretive practices make it impossible to maintain a clear or precise distinction between the two).' One would argue that these readings can be as instrumental in the creation of a fandom as the art that fans create, canonical or otherwise. Indeed, deep readings of The Hunger Games are a community-building aspect of the fandom. The *Hunger Games Fireside Chat* podcast incorporates a 'crackpot theories' feature where participants discuss possibilities of deeper readings of the canonical text. One sparked a debate about whether the Reaping of the 74th Hunger Games was rigged by the rebels. The theory states that the rebels fixed the draw in order for Prim's name to be selected. In Episode 19, the *Fireside Chat* panel discussed the possibilities surrounding this theory in detail, and many others have written about it in blogs and on fansites, asking questions like: was Primrose pre-selected as a lamb to the slaughter to unite the Districts? Was the draw rigged by the rebels knowing that Katniss would volunteer in Prim's stead? Theories like this one may sound madcap to the casual

Fig. 9: Angela Rizza's real-life
Mockingjay.

reader, but whether or not you agree with these possibilities, they are evidence of a fan base which thinks deeply and critically about the texts which are important to them.

Although exceptional readings and fan creation usually apply to fictional works which use the source text as a base to build upon, edit or recreate, there is also a place in this discussion for cultural criticism of some kinds. Indeed, many of these texts are culturally critical in their own ways, but in a direct way there are a number of fans and fan academics who are deconstructing The Hunger Games and applying their own readings to the work. Many examples are demonstrated in other essays in this book, from the gender representations to violence in the media to issues of race and disability. A key proponent of this kind of work is V. Arrow, whose 2012 book *The Panem Companion* is an impressive, all-encompassing, deep textual reading of Suzanne Collins's work. Arrow is also the co-creator of a map of Panem which went viral online. This also has offshoots as a fan by the name of Lindsay also took V. Arrow's map concept a little further and created a timeline of Panem based on The Hunger Games book series. Valerie Estelle Frankel has penned two books which delve deep into The Hunger Games: the first, *Katniss the Cattail* (2012), is an in-depth glossary of names in the series, while *The Many Faces of Katniss Everdeen: Exploring the Heroine of the Hunger Games* (2013) draws upon Collins's interactions with gender and the greater literary context out of which Katniss was born. Many more volumes have summarized the books for children, teens and adults of all ages, and explored its deeper canonical themes. But there are some fans, academic or otherwise, whose deep readings result in different modes of production and participation. The speculation within often leads to more fanciful ideas, as we'll see below.

### Non-canonical narratives

Another 'crackpot theory' on the *Fireside Chat* podcast suggested that Madge Undersee – District 12 Mayor's daughter and a friend of Katniss – escaped the bombings of District 12, travelled back in time and penned the future history of Panem under the pseudonym Suzanne Collins. On the *Fireside Chat* podcast, Episode 44, this theory was introduced for discussion by Savanna New. She asked a panelist called Kait (a contributor to *Victor's Village*) what she thought of the theory, saying 'You like to think outside the box, what do you think?' Kait promptly replied, 'I like to think outside the box, I don't like to think outside the whole universe! That's beyond the box.'

Thinking outside the box is key to the creation of interesting artwork. As we saw above, the Mockingjay symbol has captured the imaginations of many fan readers and artists, not least Angela Rizza, who pulled the idea of the Mockingjay from the story universe and placed it in the context of real life. She writes:

I haven't seen many artists interpret the Mockingjay as an actual species of bird, they

Consumption Becomes Production:
Fan Creations and *The Hunger Games*

usually present it more as an iconic symbol in The Hunger Games. I tried to reinter-
pret the original design by including some of the well known elements, but took it a
bit further making it more like a natural study. I borrowed some of the color and beak
features of a mockingbird and was inspired by the Stellar Jay for the rest.

*Fig. 10: One fan created
Katniss and Peeta's wedding
invitation.*

Another fan imagined what the marriage between Katniss the Mockingjay and Peeta
might look like. Though in the canon story the pair are engaged but never get a chance
to marry, Tumblr user Hellen, aka theinfernaldevices, mocked up her idea of a wedding
invitation. It reads, 'President Coriolanus Snow requests the honor of your presence
at the marriage of the star-crossed lovers from District 12' and that the event is 'to be
broadcast in a mandatory event'. This evokes the idea that things may have gone a different way, or that the Capitol may have been working on different ways to solve its
star-crossed lovers problem.

## 'Shipping

'Shipping is another area of fanfiction writing which is often far 'beyond the box' in
terms of what non-fans see as culturally appropriate behaviour. Existing pairings like
Katniss/Peeta (which has earned the affectionate portmanteau 'Peenis' – or, more commonly and politically correctly, 'EverLark') and Annie Cresta/Finnick Odair have been
expounded upon, but many more have been invented, too. Effie/Haymitch or 'Hayffie'
has been comically acknowledged by the actress Elizabeth Banks, who plays Effie, and
m/f (male–female) pairings like Gale/Madge, Cinna/Effie and Brutus/Enorbaria frequently appear. Like Sam Cushions music, these kinds of 'ships in fic are often an exten-
sion of the emotions and desires felt by the reader-cum-ficcer. These are also playfully
incorporated into larger narratives about coming of age and may express other latent
desires through sexually charged stories. Slashfiction (which focuses attraction and
sexual relationships between fictional characters of the same sex) is another subset of
this phenomenon, and has many iterations and subgenres of its own. For this reason,
most fanfiction has an age-appropriate rating.

   'Shipping is a form of appropriation, and one of the most visible examples of the
practice. In *Fans, Bloggers, and Gamers* (2006), Henry Jenkins puts forth that, 'Fandom
is a vehicle for marginalized sub-cultural groups (women, the young, gays, and so on) to
pry open space for their cultural concerns within dominant representations' and that
they are 'appropriating media texts and rereading them in a fashion that serves different interests'. Media like The Hunger Games are, as he puts it, 'not simply something
that can be reread [...] [but] that can and must be rewritten to make it more responsive
to their needs, to make it a better producer of personal meanings and pleasures'. One
would argue that the issue of representation is perhaps less important or stark in the
Hunger Games fandom, a text and a place which already represents women and teens.
Fans of *The Hunger Games* seem to be more exploratory, testing the limits of Suzanne

Collins's world, even relating it back to the world and cultural norms surrounding them. One fan-video maker edited together video head-shots of Jennifer Lawrence and Josh Hutcherson, clips from *The Hunger Games* movie (primarily of the two kissing) and stock wedding footage to create a narrative in which their wedding has come to pass. The fan's video asks, what if Katniss and Peeta did get married? This, in part, sates a desire to see a key romance (or 'sailed ship') come to pass. However, it is a selective reading which passes up the question of Katniss's feelings for Peeta as Part One of the saga ends, and does not ask whether or not a wedding would have gone ahead if the couple were not forced to endure more horrors at the hands of the Capitol. It expunges the heroes of their plight and provides a happy ending which is never in sight at any point throughout The Hunger Games series. Indeed, it is Annie and Finnick who are allowed to celebrate their dream wedding, though the happy moment does not linger long.

This particular example demonstrates David Bleich's findings about male and female readers, as touched upon above. In his studies of gender distinctions between readers, he found that women are generally more willing to enjoy free play with the content of stories, which included making inferences about character relationships. Men, generally, follow a pattern of reiterating the plot as information, which we'll see in Joey Graceffa's fan-video and music work below. Camille Bacon-Smith has estimated that over 90 per cent of all fan writers are female which, paired with Bleich's findings, suggests that 'shipping and fanworks like the fan-made wedding video mentioned above are not such a surprising outcome of fandom and fan creation. Men may not tend to write fanfiction, but let's look at one whose work is inspired by Suzanne Collins's and which brings the visual aspects of her dystopian tale into the sphere of popular culture and pop consumption.

## Further recreation & cultural mashups

Many of the non-canonical works like 'shipping exist in direct opposition to the canonical; however there are also scores of transformative fanworks which are non-canonical in different ways. As mentioned earlier in this chapter, pop cultural series like Honest Trailers and Bad Lip Reading parody or send-up everything from movies to politics. Other fanworks incorporate The Hunger Games into the participant's existing works and frames of reference. For example, Joey Graceffa is a prominent YouTuber and fan of The Hunger Games who, beginning with his earlier channel WinterSpringPro, made frequent music video parodies. Made in partnership with his friend Brittany, these videos also mashed up pop culture items, like their Lady Gaga 'Telephone' (2010) parody based on Chatroulette, and Game of Thrones (George R.R. Martin, 1991- ) parody using Rihanna's 'We Found Love' (2011). Graceffa took the same approach to his video for 'I Wanna Go' (2011) by Britney Spears. In this video, he plays Gale while fellow YouTubers Luke Conard and Whitney Milam play Peeta and Katniss. The lyrics refer to several aspects of the games, including Peeta's baking skills, Katniss being 'on fire' and starting a revolution. The three creators

Consumption Becomes Production:
Fan Creations and *The Hunger Games*

have also collaborated on original music based on The Hunger Games. An original song called 'The Arena' by The Tributes includes lyrics about the cameras, cannons, and silver parachutes bearing sponsor gifts. The accompanying video recreates key scenes from the Arena of the book, including the kick-off at the Cornucopia, the Careers giving chase, and Katniss dropping the Tracker Jacker nest on the Career group.

Nowadays fan videos like these can flourish online thanks to the proliferation of cheaper, easier access to film-making technology. In years past, fans would partake in the creation of fan videos which involved the editing of scenes from episodes in a series to create new narratives. Often these were created video-to-video and distributed by postal service as chain letters. In recent years it has become possible to fast-forward this process and distribute fan edits online via websites like YouTube.

Mashups are also a popular practice amongst fan editors. One fan mashed up Twilight and The Hunger Games by taking the sound from the *Hunger Games* trailer and finding moments from *Twilight* (Catherine Hardwicke, 2008) scenes to recreate the action. Though the source material is sometimes crude or ill-fitting, videos like this demonstrate the desire of some fans to combine their passions and test the limits of their abilities. Graceffa's works are also mashups of a sort, alternately bringing pop music into the storyworld of The Hunger Games and redefining the structure of the representation of that storyworld into a form which does not exist there. The clear collaboration between fan creators in Graceffa's example, and the collaboration or remixing of different cultural texts in fan editors' videos demonstrate the communities at play within the fandom. Some are disparate, brought together by the creator rather than the particular creation; others gather as peers creating their own works. Let's take a look at the communities which form over a shared enthusiasm for fan reading as creation.

## Fan creation communities
Fanfiction writers are often avid readers of their peers' creations. These fans tend to be insatiable in their love for the source story and enjoy participating in the writing of serial fics. Many also participate by reading, reviewing, and commenting on fellow ficcers' work. The peer-review process of fanfiction writing has been commended by academics studying fan participation. Henry Jenkins's essay 'Why Heather Can Write' in *Convergence Culture* looks at the immersive qualities of an apprentice education in writing through fan works. One Hunger Games fanfiction author by the LiveJournal user name kolms began the 'Girl on Fire Ficathon' on the release date of *The Hunger Games* movie, encouraging fellow fans and ficcers to participate in a drive of fanfiction writing. This played out in the comments of the instigator's blog post, with participants encouraging their fellow writers by providing prompts. From kolms's rules:

1. All pairings, 'ships, genres, AUs, gen/het/slash/fem are welcome and encouraged!
2. One prompt per comment, please, but prompt as many times as you wish.

This welcome call with well-defined yet open guidelines encouraged tens of entries and excited responses, both to the ficathon in general and to each other's work in particular. The experience once again calls to mind David Bleich's findings, as these (primarily female) readers take the practice further, throwing out ideas for participation and, in turn, complying to provide entertaining and engaging stories for others to enjoy. This is very much in the spirit of fanfiction writing, and this is a practice with a community at its heart. Indeed, if you visit any fan video with hundreds or thousands of views, the overwhelming majority of comments will be positive, share a mutual enthusiasm, and include encouraging remarks for further content. All demonstrate the strong and still-burgeoning community that is The Hunger Games fandom.

As avid fans of culture phenomena like The Hunger Games read, consume and spectate the original stories presented by Suzanne Collins, her publishers and movie rights holders, their rereading often turns into writing, their consumption into production, and their spectator culture becomes participatory culture. Fans participate in numerous ways, most prominently through discussion and evolving fan texts like fanfiction. This discussion also leads to the creation of tightknit communities who share and revel in the new stories they create. Fans have various ways to highlight and appropriate the issues and topics which are dealt with within their favourite texts, and respond in enlightening and sometimes unusual ways. Some take snapshots which they recreate through artworks while others create new narratives through stock visual images or by shooting their own recreations and interpretations. The larger popular culture surrounding The Hunger Games has also inspired spin-offs, mashups and parodies from fans and non-fans alike, each finding new ways to interact with the source text and make it more relevant to their own interests. From romances to crackpot theories, these fan reactions and modes of participation demonstrate deep readings of the source and allow for it to be recreated, crafted and defined to suit each reader. When it comes to fan participation in *The Hunger Games*, *Catching Fire* and *Mockingjay*, fire is definitely catching. ●

Consumption Becomes Production:
Fan Creations and *The Hunger Games*

~~~~~~~~~~~~~~~

## GO FURTHER

### Books

*The Many Faces of Katniss Everdeen: Exploring the Heroine of the Hunger Games*
Valerie Estelle Frankel
(Hamden, CT: Zossima Press, 2013)

*Katniss the Cattail: An Unauthorized Guide to Names and Symbols in Suzanne Collins'*
*The Hunger Games*
Valerie Estelle Frankel
(Seattle: CreateSpace Independent Publishing Platform, 2012)

*The Panem Companion: From Mellark Bakery to Mockingjays*
V. Arrow
(Dallas: Smart Pop Books, 2012)

*Convergence Culture: Where Old and New Media Collide*
Henry Jenkins
(New York: NYUP, 2008)

*Fans, Bloggers, and Gamers: Media Consumers in a Digital Age [Paperback]*
Henry Jenkins
(New York: NYUP, 2006)

*Fan Cultures*
Matt Hills
(New York: Routledge, 2002)

*Textual Poachers*
Henry Jenkins
(London: Routledge, 1992)

### Extracts/Essays/Articles

'Spock Among the Women'
Camille Bacon-Smith
*New York Times Book Review*. 16 November 1986.

'Gender Interests in Reading and Language'

David Bleich
In *Gender and Reading: Essays on Readers, Texts and Contexts*
Elizabeth A. Flynn and Patrocinio P. Schweickart
(Baltimore: Johns Hopkins University Press, 1986).

**Online**

'Transmedia Storytelling 101'
Henry Jenkins
*Confessions of an Aca-Fan.* 22 March 2007, http://henryjenkins.org/2007/03/transmedia_storytelling_101.html.

'Sam Cushion (District Tribute)'
*Down With The Capitol. [n.d.],* http://hungergamesdwtc.net/interactive/rockingjays-hunger-games-inspired-music/sam-cushion-district-tribute/.

'Episode 19'
*Hunger Games Fireside Chat.* 9 August 2011, http://www.blogtalkradio.com/firesidechat/2011/08/09/19-hunger-games-fireside-chat.

'Let's Do The Time Warp Again!'
Lindsay
*Victor's Village.* 5 October 2012,
http://victorsvillage.com/2012/10/05/lets-do-the-time-warp-again/.

'Fireside Chat #44: Look Your Best'
*Hunger Games Fireside Chat,* 31 January 2012, http://www.blogtalkradio.com/firesidechat/2012/01/31/44-fireside-chat-look-your-best.

'Josh Hutcherson's Peetaphiles & Peeniss Lovers – CONAN on TBS'
*Team Coco* [YouTube].
28 March 2012, http://www.youtube.com/watch?v=KS5BxIDQPGI#t=185.

*Websites*
*The Stacks Message Board* [Scholastic.com],
http://community.scholastic.com/hunger-games-fanfic-chapter-1-the-bloodbath-t413269.html

*Popular works*
'"The Hunger Games" – A Bad Lip Reading'

## Consumption Becomes Production:
## Fan Creations and *The Hunger Games*

*Bad Lip Reading* [YouTube]
20 September 2012, http://www.youtube.com/watch?v=QjGk_jU6t5A.

'Honest Trailers – The Hunger Games'
*Screen Junkies* [YouTube]
17 August 2012, http://www.youtube.com/watch?v=_hp_xsUg9ws.

'LITERAL The Hunger Games: Catching Fire Trailer'
*Tobuscus* [YouTube]
30 April 2013, http://www.youtube.com/watch?v=_ueJNO3-Ink

'Teens React to The Hunger Games'
*The Fine Bros* [YouTube]
18 March 2012, http://www.youtube.com/watch?v=Ri6wRz_NjiA.

'Teens React to The Catching Fire'
*The Fine Bros* [YouTube]
16 June 2013, http://www.youtube.com/watch?v=5ekoj7qfdZ4.

*Fanwork*
*The Katniss Chronicles,* http://www.thekatnisschronicles.com/

'Hunger Games – 8 Bit Cinema'
*Cinefix* [YouTube]
13 November 2013, http://www.youtube.com/watch?v=bGgTM6dgf-I.

'The Beanie Baby Hunger Games'
*The Online Musical* [YouTube]
19 March 2012, http://www.youtube.com/watch?v=N2IRxqWbTec.

'Music of Panem'
*Sam Cushion*, http://store.samcushion.com/.

'Dear Effie'
*Panem Propaganda.* 20 September 2013, http://www.panempropaganda.com/
news/2013/9/20/dear-effie-a-new-advice-column-by-effie-trinket.html.

'Celebrate Your Victors: Spotlight on Johanna Mason'
Samantha Sisson
*Panem Propaganda.* 18 September 2013, http://www.panempropaganda.com/

news/2013/9/18/celebrate-your-victors-spotlight-on-johanna-mason.html.

'Capitol Correspondence'
Aaron Darcy
*Panem Propaganda*, 20 August 2013, http://www.panempropaganda.com/
news/2013/8/20/district-4-reminder-help-feed-panem.html.

'Grow Together'
Miss Scarlett 05
*FanFiction.net*, https://www.fanfiction.net/s/6554253/1/Grow-Together.

'Commission for Branchan' (Katniss and Peeta reunite)'
*alonglineofbread* [Tumblr].
[n.d.], http://alonglineofbread.tumblr.com/post/56545893762/commission-for-bran-chan-bigger-print.

'Mockingjay Still Life'
*LaurasMuse*, http://laurasmuse.deviantart.com/art/Mockingjay-Still-Life-299978569.

'Hunger Games: The Hanging Tree'
*Mainstay Productions* [YouTube].
9 February 2013, http://www.youtube.com/watch?v=w7djN9T9Oqk.

'Hunger Games: The Second Quarter Quell'
*Mainstay Productions* [YouTube].
18 July 2011, http://www.youtube.com/watch?v=7mUjssn86h4.

'Hunger Games: Finnick and Annie Web Series'
*Mainstay Productions* [YouTube].
21 January 2012, http://www.youtube.com/watch?v=y4mrlCfOIcw.

'The Mockingjay Propo'
*Still Frame Pictures* [YouTube].
27 March 2012, http://www.youtube.com/watch?v=i8CkZhmK_Lg.

'The Hunger Games'
Kaylene / lenagurrrl
*Wattpad*, http://www.wattpad.com/story/488839-the-hunger-games.

'The Mockingjay'

**Consumption Becomes Production:
Fan Creations and *The Hunger Games***

*Angela Rizza* [Tumblr].
3 March 2012, http://angelarizza.tumblr.com/post/18700338437/mockingjay1
http://www.etsy.com/listing/94431239/the-mockingjay-8x10-print.

'We Saved Each Other'
*Hellen* [Tumblr].
19 May 2012, http://theinfernaldevices.tumblr.com/post/23365570136.

'Hunger Games Parody – "I Wanna Go" (Britney Spears)'
*WinterSpringPro* [YouTube].
29 September 2013, http://www.youtube.com/watch?v=rNZ6DOYOYCc.

'HUNGER GAMES MUSIC VIDEO! "THE ARENA" – The Tributes'
*Joey Graceffa et al.* [YouTube].
21 March 2012, http://www.youtube.com/watch?v=WD24tWfMoR8.

'The Twilight Saga (Hunger Games Style)'
*Bombonrosa* [YouTube].
1 August 2012, http://www.youtube.com/watch?v=altef79EOiQ.

'Girl on Fire Ficathon'
*kolms* [LiveJournal].
23 March 2013, http://kolms.livejournal.com/18020.html.

*Fansites*
*Hunger Games Fireside Chat*, http://www.hgfiresidechat.com

# CLOSING MY EYES DOESN'T HELP. FIRE BURNS BRIGHTER IN THE DARKNESS.

**KATNISS EVERDEEN**
MOCKINGJAY

# Author Biography

AUTHOR

**Nicola Balkind** is a writer and digital freelancer based in Glasgow, Scotland. She is the editor of *World Film Locations: Glasgow* (Intellect Books, 2013) and contributes to a number of books, blogs and the BBC Radio Scotland's Culture Studio. You can find Nicola online at http://nicolabalkind.com and on Twitter *@robotnic*.

# Image Credits

Front Inside Flap @ Steven Murphee & Karen Parris / Still Frame Pictures
Back Inside Flap @ Harry Potter Alliance

Chapter 1    Fig. 1, p. 9 @ Victoria Will / AP
             Fig. 2, p. 10 @ Murray Close / Lionsgate
             Fig. 3, p. 10 @ Murray Close / Lionsgate
             Fig. 4, p. 12 @ Jesse aka lilyart, http://lilyart.deviantart.com
             Fig. 5, p. 15 @ Murray Close / Lionsgate
Chapter 2    Fig. 1, p. 19 @ palnk, http://palnk.deviantart.com
             Fig. 2, p. 20 @ Murray Close / Lionsgate
             Fig. 3, p. 22 @ Lionsgate
             Fig. 4, p. 24 @ Emma, http://catching-smoke.deviantart.com
Chapter 3    Fig. 1, p. 39 @ http://shadowsgallery.tumblr.com
             Fig. 2, p. 41@ Murray Close / Lionsgate
             Fig. 3, p. 43 @ Murray Close / Lionsgate
             Fig. 4, p. 44 @ Sabine Sennert-Wrede, Mainstay Productions
Chapter 4    Fig. 1, p. 52 @ Lionsgate / Lionsgate
             Fig. 2, p. 55 @ CoverGirl
             Fig. 3, p. 55 @ http://www.mockingjay.net
Chapter 5    Fig. 1, p. 72 @ Lidia, http://skinku-chan.deviantart.com
             Fig. 2, p. 73 @ Edited by http://ghostofharrenhal.tumblr.com
             Fig. 3, p. 73 @ Internet meme, author unknown
             Fig. 4, p. 76 @ Internet meme, author unknown
             Fig. 5, p. 76 @ Internet meme, author unknown
Chapter 6    Fig. 1, p. 84 @ Lionsgate, Feeding America and World Food Programme
             Fig. 2, p. 85 @ Harry Potter Alliance
             Fig. 3, p. 88 @ Fanwork, author unknown
Chapter 7    Fig. 1, p. 102 @ The Hunger Games RPG, http://www.thehungergamesrpg.com
             Fig. 2, p. 103 @ Explore Asheville, http://www.exploreasheville.com
             Fig. 3, p. 104 @ Cyndi Hoelzle
             Fig. 4, p. 105 @ Amanda Bell
             Fig. 5, p. 106 @ Margo Metzger, http://www.visitnc.com; Murray Close/Lionsgate
Chapter 8    Fig. 1, p. 111 @ Panem October, author unknown
             Fig. 2, p. 112 @ Panem October, author unknown
             Fig. 3, p. 113 @ Panem October, author unknown
             Fig. 4, p. 115 @ The Capitol PN / Lionsgate
Chapter 9    Fig. 1, p. 135 @ Mainstay Productions
             Fig. 2, p. 135 @ The Online Musical
             Fig. 3, p. 137 @ Samantha Sisson / Panem Propaganda
             Figs. 4-7, p.138 @ http://alonglineofbread.tumblr.com
             Fig. 8, p. 140 @ V. Arrow
             Fig. 9, p. 141 @ Angela Rizza
             Fig. 10, p. 142 @ Helen, http://theinfernaldevices.tumblr.com

# SO AFTER,
# WHEN HE WHISPERS,
# 'YOU LOVE ME.
# REAL OR NOT REAL?'
# I TELL HIM,
# 'REAL.'

**KATNISS EVERDEEN**
**MOCKINGJAY**

# FAN PHENOMENA

OTHER TITLES AVAILABLE IN THE SERIES

**Star Trek**
Edited by Bruce E. Drushel
ISBN: 978-1-78320-023-8
£15.50 / $22

**Star Wars**
Edited by Mika Elovaara
ISBN: 978-1-78320-022-1
£15.50 / $22

**The Big Lebowski**
Edited by Zachary Ingle
ISBN: 978-1-78320-202-7
£15.50 / $22

**The Big Lebowski**
Edited by Lynn Zubernis
and Katherine Larsen
ISBN: 978-1-78320-203-4
£15.50 / $22

**Doctor Who**
Edited by Paul Booth
ISBN: 978-1-78320-020-7
£15.50 / $22

**Buffy the Vampire Slayer**
Edited by Jennifer K. Stuller
ISBN: 978-1-78320-019-1
£15.50 / $22

**Twin Peaks**
Edited by Marisa C. Hayes
and Franck Boulegue
ISBN: 978-1-78320-024-5
£15.50 / $22

**Audrey Hepburn**
Edited by Jacqui Miller
ISBN: 978-1-78320-206-5
£15.50 / $22

For further information about the series
and news of forthcoming titles visit **www.intellectbooks.com**